POWER

Your Potential BOOST CAMP

LEADERSHIP EDITION

Dr. Valerie D.W. James

POWER

Your Potential BOOST CAMP

LEADERSHIP EDITION

7 Days to Professional Success and Satisfaction!

Dr. Valerie D. W. James

Solutions **M**aximizing **B**rilliance
SMB School of Leadership BOOST CAMP®

A Division of VisionSpot Consulting Group LLC

POWER to THRIVE BOOST CAMP Publishing Company

Copyright © 2008, reprint 2018

ISBN: 978-0-97-98973-1-3

Cover design and photo by Marcus Redd Mediaworks

Published in the United States of America

Enhance Your *POWER* to THRIVE!®

Decide Commit Achieve™

[handwritten: Malaysia Your Mission is Possible too! To Your Success... (signature)]

What others are saying about **POWER** Your Potential
BOOST CAMP ...

"I truly enjoyed reading the **POWER** *Your Potential BOOST CAMP Leadership Edition. This book gave me even more valuable insight and information to use as a road map for my career as a new leader."*

N'Chelle Norris, Executive Assistant, Toyota North America

"Picture someone receiving a tool at just the right moment in their life that will take them beyond their dreams and expectations. Dr. Valerie's **POWER** *Your Potential BOOST CAMP new Leadership Edition: 7 Days to Professional Success and Satisfaction, is that tool!"*

J. Eldridge Taylor Jr., President, The J. Eldridge Taylor Co.

Dedication

─────

To <u>*S*</u>*ir,* <u>M</u>*ichelle and* <u>B</u>*randon*

My three heartbeats above inspired the solution *that helped
me* maximize *my* brilliance *personally and professionally, and as a
leader. I thank all three of you for allowing me to be mom, mentor,
confidant, example, and coach personally and professionally. It is
my hope that you will have the courage to face life's journey with a
Mission Possible philosophy and a commitment that embodies the
principles of God's divine word and the unique gifts discovered as
you continue POWERing your potential to do great things.*

Love always, Mom
(Your Sunshine)

Disclaimer

────────

This book is designed to provide information on how to reveal your innate abilities by leading you to a more fulfilling career. It is sold with the understanding that the publisher and author are not engaged in rendering legal, accounting, or other professional services. If legal or other expert assistance is required, the services of a competent professional should be sought. The purpose of this book is not to reprint all the information that is otherwise available to individuals and/or organizations, but instead to complement, amplify, and supplement other texts. You are urged to read all of the available material to learn as much as possible about personal and professional development, and tailor the information to your individual needs.

The *POWER Your Potential BOOST CAMP® Leadership Edition: 7 Days to Professional Success and Satisfaction* is not a get-rich-quick scheme. Anyone who decides to enhance his or **POWER** her current career potential or forge into new professional territory by using this book must expect to invest time and effort. For many people, change is good and allows them to grow and prosper doing work they not only enjoy, but also can do extremely well. Every effort has been made to make this book

Table of Contents

Introduction

Your Career Deserves a BOOST!

There is nothing more professionally satisfying than reaching your true potential and doing work that brings you satisfaction at the end of the day and at the end of a decade. When we are not in touch with our own talents and desires, it is all too easy to settle for a job that is "close enough" or to feel stuck in unsatisfying careers. Whether you are in your ideal career and wish to remain, know what you want to do or you just know that you want a change, the ***POWER*** *Your Potential BOOST CAMP* will help you develop all the tools you need to achieve your true professional potential.

You have heard of boot camps-the goal being to break you down and build you back up. In the ***POWER*** *Your Potential BOOST CAMP*, it is all about building you up based on the best of who you really are. This is not about changing yourself to get into a job that you do not really want. This is about developing a mindset that will give you an upward push. **Think of the word BOOST as a mobilizing language for rising higher.** With my help, you are going to give yourself a great big BOOST by tapping into your true self and allowing that authenticity to ***POWER*** *Your Potential* to excel in the career of your dreams, using effective, yet motivational techniques that will guide you to your next level.

This new leadership edition will take you step by step through the **POWER** *Your Potential BOOST CAMPS,* supporting you in identifying your personal brand of leadership and create a safety nest for your career by becoming better acquainted with your professional needs and truest talents.

You will learn how to do the following:

- Redirect or reinvent a stagnant career
- Pinpoint your strengths and style then use them to overcome barriers to entry into your desired profession
- Develop the confidence you need to step boldly into the next level of your career
- Set and achieve goals using a comprehensive system that really works

Prepare yourself to be pleasantly surprised when you discover the full range of your potential as you learn to tap into your real **POWER,** which is your personal strength, might and an internal force that gives you the capability to do or accomplish something grand.

We all deserve to pursue our dreams for a successful future. Reaching your potential is a great gift to yourself and to the entire world. The best part about the **POWER** *Your Potential BOOST CAMP* is that you can start wherever you are today and build from there. The exercises in this book are designed to guide you in your journey toward self-discovery and professional success. By completing the exercises with intention and thought, you will learn what steps are needed to **"POWER** Your Potential" and successfully achieve your goals.

Professional development programs are essential in today's world because your options are truly limitless. It is only when you tune into yourself, your needs, and your talents that you can identify your true professional path. You will make real changes only when you feel deep down in your gut that it is time. In this book you will be challenged to take your career to the next level by helping you focus and set your sights on your specific and personalized goals. It is only when you are headed in the right direction that your efforts will lead you to a place of deeply satisfying professional success.

This book was born out of my passion to help others bring out their hidden talents, develop unshakable confidence, and awaken the unique ability within to **POWER** your potential to THRIVE. Each of us should be able to speak to our own attributes and contributions as if we are describing our most admired person. Most people are uncomfortable speaking about themselves, nevertheless I am going to help you get clear about your personal value and teach you how to become the Chief Empowerment Officer (CEO) of your career. My personal story is courageously told at the onset of this book as a glimpse of just how these concepts are rooted into the fabric of my **DNA.**

Believe it or not, every one of us is an entrepreneur with a product to sell and a service to offer. Your skills, talents, and experiences are your product, and your level of performance is your service. The way you present these attributes has a great impact on your ability to reach your potential, hence giving you the **POWER** to change from ordinary to *extraordinary* in seven days.

The simple and straightforward exercises in the ***POWER*** *Your Potential BOOST CAMPS* are designed to spark new ideas and insights. In one short week, you will begin to think differently and more enthusiastically about yourself and the **POWER** within you to take action.

On DAY 1, you will complete several proven assessments to help you identify your professional skills and accomplishments and present them in a way that really impresses employers and clients. On DAY 2, you will dream BIG so you can enlarge your vision for what's possible in your life. On DAY 3, you will start renovating your belief system, clearing out limiting beliefs, and instilling positive and inspiring thoughts that will allow you to be your own best resource.

On DAY 4, you will create S.M.A.R.T. **POWER** goals and a mission statement. On DAY 5, you will learn to develop your dream support network. On DAY 6, you will learn tips for taking care of your greatest asset (that being YOU!). Finally, on DAY 7, you will develop a plan to put everything you have learned and achieved into action so that you can take the steps needed to reach your full professional potential.

The last section, Life after **BOOST CAMP,** will offer encouragement and guidance for continuing your action plan until your goals are reached. With regular review and repetition, your unique potential will be revealed and positive affirmations you have written in this book will become second nature to you as you continually Give Yourself a **POWERfull** BOOST.

You are encouraged to take in the information you learn during this BOOST CAMP experience and relate it to your life personally and professionally, always keeping in mind both the life you have and the life you want. This book is developed for people who have a burning desire to take the lid off of their life and develop a path that aligns with what matters most in their career. However, you must be coachable and willing to do the work. The information learned can be a source of inspiration and excitement. After working through the exercises and steps of the ***POWER*** *Your Potential BOOST CAMP,* you will reach your true professional potential and your life will never be the same. You will become the official CEO of your career while working in corporate America. In seven days you will gain knowledge of the fact that the **POWER** to succeed is already within you-you were born with it and it will always be a part of who you are. You simply need to learn how to harness that **POWER** and apply it toward achieving your potential.

As you begin this exciting and life-changing program, write in the margins any thoughts that come to mind. Make notes to help you remember key points or highlight important trigger words, concepts or phrases. Most importantly, "Give Yourself a "**BOOST**" by committing right now to complete all the sections in the book. Every time you need an energy BOOST to get you going again, say to yourself, it is all about me right now!" *Yes, it is all about the POWER within you to* **THRIVE!** I wish you lots of joy and enthusiasm as you embark on the adventure of achieving your greatest professional potential!

Dr. Valerie D. W. James
Your Partner in Success
VisionSpot Consulting Group, LLC

Courageous Story of Success

"To experience success, you must become a master of the "Win-Win" attitude."

-Robb D. Thompson

I have spent an enormous amount of time capturing and verbalizing this innovative approach to **POWER** Your Potential to THRIVE. As a glimpse of just how these concepts are rooted into the fabric of my **DNA,** I would like to share with you my personal journey towards self-discovery. Using the very steps in this program, I have managed to identify my true professional calling—which includes working with people like you in their quest to achieve their true potential. By pursuing this calling, I have achieved a great deal of professional success and personal satisfaction. My journey toward realizing my own leadership potential has been a long and difficult one, however, it was worth every second of time and ounce of effort to get here. I learned that success and satisfaction were, and still are determined by how I choose to use each minute of every day. I would like to share a bit about my experiences with you, to serve as inspiration and proof that real transformation can happen in a matter of days, *but you have to be willing to do the work!*

I was one of the most professional-looking students in my high school. I wore blazers with my slacks or dresses and carried a briefcase or portfolio instead of a backpack every day for my books and note pads. I was on time to every class and I worked in the administrative office to get extra credit. It gave me a sense of value. I looked like I had it all together, the epitome of success!

MY SECRET

However, on the inside I was harboring a very embarrassing secret. I also had very low self-esteem, which in turn had a direct effect on my ability to do well in other areas of my life. For Example: when I graduated high school, I had a challenge with reading that affected my spelling and comprehension. Despite receiving a high school diploma, I read at a seventh-grade reading level and my reading comprehension was at a fifth grade level. I was too embarrassed to share my weaknesses in these areas, for fear of being labeled "dumb" or "slow." I just remember my six grade teacher Mrs. Hamilton calling me "*The little engine that could*". By the time I sounded out all the words in a sentence, I lost the thread of its message and had to start from the beginning. I did not know at the time that I was dyslexic. Dyslexia is not reversing letters, as most people may think. Dyslexia is when someone has difficulty isolating the sounds within a spoken word and then attaching the appropriate letter to the sound. It affected my ability to rapidly retrieve the words I wanted to say and to read fluently. It is considered a learning disability (Weakness within the functional part of the brain where the sounds of language are put together to form words and where words are broken down into sound). Through further research, I found out that I was not alone in my struggles, that dyslexia was also associated with someone having high intelligence, and some of the most brilliant minds in history had dyslexia. For Example: Albert Einstein,

Alexander Graham Bell, Thomas Edison, Winston Churchill, Benjamin Franklin, General George Patton to name a few.

Being raised as an only child, acceptance and feeling inclusive were very important to me. My parents were great supporters, motivators and very nurturing. However, they were not aware of my reading challenges, I was able to maintain good grades by learning to visualize the ideas presented in class, by reading things over and over again, or by having phone conversations with other classmates about the topic to hear their views on the subject.

In an attempt to improve my reading skills, I circled every word I encountered that I could not pronounce and looked it up in the dictionary. In doing this I discovered that the words I had circled were actually ones I already used on a daily basis. I had just never seen them written down. It was an emotionally frustrating struggle because the reading challenge also affected my ability to spell. However, the dictionary was a great tool, because it broke down the words into syllables and gave guidance about a word's pronunciation. I also watched educational programs on television, even those for small children, which also helped me develop and enhance my reading and comprehension skills.

Every summer I visited my grandparents Lewis and Leola Davis and Aunt Tee in Mobile, Alabama. There I was guaranteed some of my grandmother's famous biscuits and good food, lots of hugs and kisses; playtime with the twins who lived across the street and roller coaster rides with my cousin Andretta in the back of my grandfather's station wagon. My other grandparents were also loving and kind, but extremely conservative. You see, my grandfather Henry. L Williams was a former principal and superintendent in the Clarke County public school system. My grandmother Mattye J. Williams (affectionately known as Dear) was a teacher and former principal as well. She is sweet as pie, but she is very serious when it comes to "getting your lesson," as she calls it. I loved going to their house as well, but I knew that one of the prerequisites during the visit would be to complete reading, writing, and arithmetic lessons in a workbook before watching television or going out to play and she modeled that behavior as well. As you can see, to top it off, she dedicated an entire wall in the family room of their house to academic achievement. My ultimate measure of success was to be smart enough to make the wall!

My grandmother Dear is 92 years young and still leading by example.

Dear's academic achievements wall

My grandmother wanted to ensure that I did not lose too much discipline and academic focus over the summer vacation. At that time, I HATED IT! But I APPRECIATE every bit of it today. My cousin Cosandra and I still laugh and joke about how strict she was along with the values of her guiding principles.

THE HEART OF DETERMINATION

It was important for me to not only look successful, but I also wanted to feel the success on the inside. Although I did not have the confidence I needed at that time I did have a determined heart to achieve something grand. I went to a community college right out of high school. I wanted to be an achiever of great things, speak with elegance and read with better clarity so that I could gain the knowledge I needed to help me THRIVE as a tried and true professional. I really wanted that, but it was tough. The lectures in college were way over my head. I felt lost and out of place, so I stopped going.

Prior to landing my first big corporate job, I worked in a beauty salon as a receptionist, in the family car business as a secretary, and at high-end retail stores as a sales clerk and co-manager. These were great stepping-stones that gave me the opportunity to develop and understand key concepts such as diversity, inclusion, teamwork, leadership, and high-quality service. However, when I began applying for jobs in the corporate arena, I always limited myself to entry-level positions because of my literacy challenges. I feared making mistakes on paperwork and I feared I would expose my deficiencies during conversations with top-ranking professionals. Even after I worked in a few front office positions following my retail career, I kept assuming that I was not good enough for anything more.

Before I learned how to **POWER** my potential to THRIVE, I had never taken into consideration my experiences and achievements along the way. At that time, I did not realize that dressing for success in middle and high school, completing those workbook assignments at Dear's house and working in the school administrative office would really payoff one day. Overtime my ability to visualize concepts in my head became a valuable transferable skill. The skills developed in the workplace helped me become more disciplined and offered value in the next phase of my professional journey as well.

During my process of self-discovery, I realized that I needed to isolate myself when I read. Another important element of my focus was organization. Before I opened a book or started on a project, I organized or removed any perceived distraction around me, such as: desk toys, other notes, pictures, bills, the phone, moving people, or the television. I developed a system that offered incremental opportunities for achievements along the way. I also realized that reading in the early morning hours worked best because I did not have the events of my day crowding my head. Late nights after a bath also worked well because I was more relaxed. Through better understanding of my body energy level and peak performance level, I was able to focus better.

Through my struggle, I allowed myself to be drawn to intelligent people, because I saw in them a mirror of what I needed to do to become the person I wanted to be and to realize my true potential. The people I most admired for their intelligence seemed to have a very optimistic attitude, took on more responsibilities, rarely complained, had a willingness to share their insights, and exhibited an embracing attitude toward differences among people. They asked questions, tried new things and welcomed constructive advice. The feedback not only posed a challenge, but also afforded them the ability to continuously raise the bar. Although reaching the top mark was always their goal, they knew that everyone had the potential to bring something valuable to the table. They appeared to be go-getters with a *Mission Possible* attitude, very confident, fearless, authentic, generous and prosperous.

Although my parents and family members made some great ethical deposits in my life, the two people whose congeniality and intellect impressed me most were my grandmother Dear and my Aunt Ardean D. Turnbull. My grandmother has a passion for people development and has been teaching for more than fifty years. She has a number of degrees, including two master's degree in Education and other professional certifications and humanitarian awards, all of which she achieved as a wife and mother. As mentioned, she was also a substitute teach in the Mobile, Alabama school district until the age 91 years young, and would still be working today if they called her at age 92. She is famous for contributing countless hours volunteering her time, talents and support throughout the community.

My Aunt Ardean was the first young person I knew who went to college. She made it appear to be the coolest thing to do. Through her life I actually saw the real benefits of "making the grades" and the true meaning of the saying "Knowledge is **POWER.**" After she graduated from college, her new residence was in St. Thomas, U.S. Virgin Islands, one of America's top vacation spots. She landed a job working for the Department of Human Services, where she served in several upwardly mobile positions with commitment, dedication and distinction. She is a great planner, organizer and leader and is still the family's "human encyclopedia." If she set a goal, you better believe she was going to achieve it. If you asked her something and she didn't know the answer, she would find out.

During my summer vacations to Mobile, Alabama, to my grandparents' Lewis and Leola's house, I slept in my aunt's room and looked at her pictures from college over and over again. It has been said that pictures are worth a thousand words. Well, let me tell you she had hundreds of them. Every year, gazing at them was a part of my summer ritual. In those pictures it looked like she was having a great deal of fun. She was the personification of intelligence, very giving, and just plain had it all together personally and professionally.

My Aunt has traveled a lot with her family and is one of the most generous members of our family. I observed how Ardean would surround herself with positive people and was very confident in her ability to complete even the most challenging task. She is always willing to lend a helping hand. I admired these traits, and subconsciously, I began emulating them. I am sure if you sit back and think about your yesteryears you will be able to come up with one or two of these people in your journey as well.

Although I had great examples of the good and not so good all around me, I did not know anything about mentors and protegees until I became an adult. I doubted myself at times. However, I felt in my heart that one day I would be successful just like those I had admired. I had always been amazed at other people's abilities and felt that everyone else was better than me. Over time I noticed that my family, colleagues, and friends were crediting me with actually having many of the same traits I had been admiring in others. Over time I began to appreciate and value my naturally creative talents and caring heart. I started to feel more **emPOWERed** and more optimistic about my chances for reaching my ultimate potential.

PUTTING A DEMAND ON MY POTENTIAL

I remember the interview for my first big corporate position as if it happened yesterday. I woke up feeling a little nervous, but I was also very excited. I got out of bed and headed for the shower. At that moment something inside of me said, "Be bold! Be strong! You can choose to have a **POWER-filled** day or a piti-filled day. You have what it takes, Valerie. Stop doubting yourself." I got in the shower and mentally washed off the fears festering inside of me. I was sick and tired of my highest goal being a comfort level of bare minimums, hoping and wishing for a bigger payoff one day, yet believing it could not happen for little old me. I knew I had to change my limited thinking and put a demand on my potential. If I wanted the person interviewing me to believe in me, I had to walk in the door with a new boldness believing in myself.

I walked into the interview room with my head up-not my normal posture at that time-feeling ready and energetic. I discussed and sold my attributes and skills developed in my previous position as if I were describing my favorite designer label. As I heard myself speak, I began to impress myself. The reality-based positive self-talk gave me the **BOOST** I needed to remove any anxiety I had about my limitations. For the first time ever, I walked away from an interview feeling really good about myself, and all of the strategies I practiced are outlined in this book.

Two weeks later, I accepted the position. I began working for a Fortune 500 communications company as the sales secretary to one of the highest-ranking managers in the company. I knew very little about the corporate world, but I was determined to make the best of my opportunity. During my new hire orientation and training, I established relationships with some great people who took me under their wings and became my trusted advisers. My people skills and core values, developed from childhood, became a valuable transferable skill that sparked successful relationship on the job. My colleagues were drawn to me because of my enthusiastic spirit, my determination, and my promising potential. At times, they could see that I was having some challenges and offered a helping hand or recommendations to get me up to speed. Working for that company turned out to be the best ten years of my professional journey.

THE TURNING POINT

Although I longed to further my education, I soon realized that the on-the-job experience would BOOST my self-confidence and help me develop intellectually and professionally in a diverse working environment. After less than two years working for a Fortune 500 communications company, I was promoted to a supervisory position. As I moved up the ranks, my new manager, another wonderful teacher, often assigned me tasks outside of my comfort zone. Those assignments challenged me to think BIG which allowed my creativity and decision-making skills to come to life. I slowly gained comfort in formulating strategies for organizational improvement, leading task teams for office mergers, staffing, and event planning; my responsibilities expanded, soon I was creating administrative budgets. I was even designing and implementing retention and employee development and recognition programs. Yes, little old ME!

Although, I was a visionary thinker and could eloquently verbalize the concepts developed for a project, I continued to have difficulty putting the details in writing, until I learned the true art of inclusion and the value of diversity. Having a great network of people with diverse skills and a team of individuals with whom I could collaborate became invaluable. I learned to work around my weak points and allow those with the strengths I lacked to do what they did best, while I did what I did best. This approach allowed everyone to put forth greater efforts in the areas where they were strong (Teamwork and inclusion).

Later in my career, one of my managers gave me a professional development and skills inventory worksheet. I looked at it and felt as though I did not have anything to put on paper.

The worksheet enabled me to identify each of the steps I needed to take to achieve my goals. It was one of the hardest assignments I had ever received. Completing the section in the skills inventory worksheet forced me to develop a benchmark for where I was currently verses where I wanted to be in my career, experience and education. I also developed action steps to make the goals real and learned to celebrate "me" throughout the process. Yes, at first I thought I did not have anything to put on the paper, but when I got serious, it took only a week to put my goals down clearly. Thanks to the clarity of vision that the assignment afforded me, I finally did it. Through regular review and planning I began by reaching several of the goals I had set. Those incremental achievements offered gratification, which motivated me to continue. Every time I was able to highlight a task as completed, I became more motivated and my confidence increased. I got so excited; I made a commitment to my staff to assist them with their personal development and career goals (I know for sure a few of them admittedly HATED IT, but they APPRECIATED it later). As part of their commitment I recommended that they complete a similar worksheet. I held morning coffee talk meetings to discuss their personal goals in conjunction with the departmental goals. I followed up by conducting one-on-one meetings to hone in on individual interests, values, and strengths. They learned from me, and I learned from them as well.

I often had discussions with my former boss, Charles Anderson, who later became my lifelong mentor, about my desire to go back to school. He encouraged me and advised me to start with one class at a time, ideally starting with something I was really interested in to help keep me motivated. The company we worked for offered tuition reimbursement. For my class enrollment to be fully compensated, I was required to achieve a grade of "B" or better, but my **S.M.A.R.T.** goal was a grade no less than an "A." I was ready! The task required a significant time commitment and a lot of effort, but I was ready to take flight.

I shared my desire to return to school with my husband and children. They supported what would be a little disruption in our everyday routine to support my dream. My husband became Mr. Mom, and my children took on the roles of independent soldiers around the house. I registered for two classes: Introduction to Business Law and Accounting 101. I had a true passion for the law but studying balance sheets gave me nightmares. However, it was in an area I needed to learn. The classes were challenging, but I felt good being there and I fell in love with learning. I start reading, writing and volunteering to speak more and the on-the-job experience helped ease the pressure of trying to relate to topics discussed. Needless to say, going back to school was one of the best decisions I had ever made. I was working, slowly but surely, toward reaching my true potential. Nothing had ever felt better. My family and I often reminisce about the experience today.

With the help of my husband, I carefully developed a workable regimen for attending classes that included a balance of family, work, self-care, and school. There were times when I wanted to give up, especially after being hospitalized with an illness. An outpatient surgery turned into two more surgeries and the nuisance of rehabilitation therapy because of a doctor's mistake was enough to make a superhero quit.

To my dismay, there were people with whom I had close connections who criticized my effort, laughed at the thought of me accomplishing my dreams, and strongly discredited my ability to achieve them. Although it hurt, I instantly turned that negative energy and pain into a positive force and persevered. My drive to be an example for my children and family and to prove the others wrong pushed me to beat the odds. In less than two years I graduated with my Associate's degree in Interdisciplinary Studies. It felt great! That success encouraged me to set my sights high and make a personal commitment to myself to keep going and believe wholeheartedly in my ability to **POWER** my full potential for the rest of my future.

While I continued to work toward my undergraduate degree, professionally I was either promoted or honored with awards for leadership. In less than three years, I had accomplished every one of my goals, including becoming a more confident reader and speaker, earning a bachelor's degree in Business Management and obtaining a leadership position at work.

Perhaps the best part about going to school while working in my chosen field was meeting some great like-minded and results-driven people. I was able to immediately apply the lessons learned in class to my everyday work and share them with my staff while adding value to the organization. As a result, my work centers had the lowest turnover rate in the company and the highest number of promotions. In the ten years with that company I had professionally coached and mentored hundreds of people. Thirteen of my subordinates and more than seven non-departmental mentees moved into leadership positions. Over eighteen recruits were promoted to advanced levels within the organization. Over half received formal recognition for their commitment to team excellence or extraordinary leadership and service to the company.

The challenging task of juggling a leadership career, a rich family life, and a second career as a full-time student, paid off. My reading, writing, and comprehension skills dramatically improved, and I had earned my bachelor's degree. Shortly after I completed my degree, the company announced that it would be closing down its local offices and centralizing operations in Salt Lake City, Utah, a move I was not in a position to make at the time. With my degree and my new Mission Possible philosophy, I was ready to spread my wings and go it alone. I walked away from my professional leadership career in communications to help other people become more successful. I founded my own company, VisionSpot Consulting, a professional training and development firm, which evolved from a college business international marketing paper, that I wrote.

The formative phase of VisionSpot Consulting, LLC was productive for me. But prior to launching my consulting firm, I was offered an opportunity to work as a sales representative for a well-known pharmaceutical company. The position provided me with the flexibility of working from home and included great perks. I cleaned out my briefcase, packed up my suits, shined my shoes, and went on my way to a three-week training and certification program that would change my life-just not in the way I thought it would at the time. After going through a grueling three-week crash course in medicine, I did not pass the certification requirements, and I was let go. I was devastated. It took me back to my earlier years, and at first I wanted to crawl back into my old shell of self-doubt.

Guess what? The temporary setback became a blessing. The time off allowed me to spend special quality time with my family. I was also able to revisit and update my career inventory worksheet, and think hard about what I really wanted out of life. I knew I had no control over when I came into this world or when my last day will be, but I did have control over how I could live my best life "in the dash." I knew that if I wanted others to continue believing in me, I had to start believing in myself again. Instead of focusing on what I had not achieved, slowly but surely, I focused on the things I knew how to do well and told myself each day, " I am going to make today a great day." Then I set out to make my desires come true. Sometimes we all have to go back to the basics in an effort to move far beyond the fundamentals to succeed.

Imagine a pitcher on a baseball field. Before he throws the ball, he must first get in to position, step back, and then lunge forward to make that pitch successful. If he tries something new and it does not work, the next time he has to reposition himself to win. In life, every time we want to stretch far beyond the basics to reach higher, we have to step back evaluate, reposition ourselves, then lunge forward to become more successful.

What initially appeared to be the worst thing that ever happened to me in my career became one of the best things that ever happened. Following that experience, I put my heart and soul into developing my practice. At the same time, I enrolled into graduate school and went to work for another Fortune 500 financial company in administration and human resources. I saw this as a means to gain more professional diversity on my resume and earn money for my business while still honoring my family commitments. During that exciting time, I received a Hall of Fame award for leadership. As a leader in human resources, one of my most pivotal roles was mediating relationships between leaders and their employees. In that role, I experienced firsthand the cost of ineffective leadership, inclusion and communication breakdowns, and the rewards of improving those areas, which gave birth to my passion for studying leadership. Instead of congregating with others around the water cooler talking about what wasn't right about leaders and the organization, I helped create the change that we wish to see in the world of work by working to change the face of leadership. This began my passion of developing a way to transform an ordinary day at work into an extraordinary day at work.

Now I am the CEO of a thriving consulting company and the Principal of the traveling leadership school, which offers popular BOOST CAMPs that are designed to teach individuals, leaders and their teams how to achieve extraordinary results. I live with the deep satisfaction that I am continually learning, growing and succeeding at reaching my ultimate potential. With every goal that I attain, I am excited to know there are more goals that I can achieve. Today, I'm happy to share with you that I have earned a Doctorate of Education in Organizational Leadership from Pepperdine University and numerous professional credentials from Harvard and some of the most prestigious universities in California. Most importantly, I do work that I truly enjoy, work that allows me to reach my true potential each and every day and pay it forward.

I attribute my success in **POWERing** my potential to THRIVE personally and professionally to identifying my unique talents, higher learning and my limitless ability to persevere with confidence. Becoming a sponge while working in corporate America was a big value as well.

When other people were complaining about having to do more, I took the opportunity to learn something new and took on extra responsibilities. I asked questions, observed things done incorrectly and made a conscious effort not to make the same mistakes. When my manager praised something, I did more for additional encouragement. I embraced change and challenged myself to think outside the box when it came to my capabilities and values. I kept a file of all accolades for my good and not-so-good days.

I pulled from the wisdom of others and utilized leadership skills acquired and positively encouraged and credited employees at every level for any task they did that demonstrated their true potential. I swallowed my pride and asked others for constructive feedback. I also shared my professional aspirations with my managers and requested their support in helping me attain my goals, although there were no guarantees of in-house advancement. Fortunately for me, not one manager denied me support when asked. I not only worked for the company, but the company worked for me and the same can happen for you as well.

As a result of my devotion to completing the activities in this book, commitment to higher learning, drive for excellence, and perseverance, I made my grandmother Dear's wall! In spite of the odds, I did it! What's even more inspiring, I am the only doctor on her wall!

My own wall of academic accolades

Yes, "*the little engine that could*" in Mrs. Hamilton's six grade class now has her own wall of academic achievements to be proud of as well. I am also elated to share that I am a Harvard trained leader and my family, colleagues, customers and managers now refer to me as "Dr. Valerie".

That is my story. What is your story and ultimate measure of success? I wrote this book to share all of the steps I followed along the path of my own leadership career journey. With the proper support, desire and dedication towards doing the work everyone can learn to **POWER** his or her own leadership potential. I believe in your ability to **POWER** your true potential, and it is my life's work to help you get there.

Leadership BOOST

Any leadership expert can tell you, leading others begins with taking a personal inventory of your own strengths and weaknesses and then assessing the opportunities and threats that are likely to present themselves as you lead. True leaders emerge by constantly taking stock of where they are and where they want to go. That is why on-going personal and professional development is vital. Everyone has the potential to be a leader. *POWER Your Potential BOOST CAMP® Leadership Edition: 7 Days to Professional Success and Satisfaction,* this concept is described as the capacity to exercise choice and autonomy in your professional journey. True leadership emerges when you develop a career path that allows you to walk in your strength to deliver results you are capable and willing to transfer to the world of work. Whenever you take the initiative to get something accomplished in your life, you are practicing leadership at the grass roots level, even if you are only leading yourself. The key to a successful leadership career is to develop behavior approaches that are authentic and that differentiate "your business" from another, by searching for the core of what you have to offer. Great leaders display strong personal values and seek new ways to demonstrate the values they have for themselves and others.

In *POWER Your Potential BOOST CAMP® Leadership Edition: 7 Days to Professional Success and Satisfaction*, I teach people how to become the CEO (Chief Empowerment Officer) of their career. It is believed that most extraordinary leaders are not born, but made. Whether you are a leader of the fortune 100 organization or the CEO of one person (self), true leadership begins with a thorough self-evaluation. If the idea of leading yourself sounds odd, think about this: your unique set of skills and personal attributes are your product and the way you utilize those special qualities will make your name and professional brand stand out, get noticed, and be remembered and rewarded for its unique characteristics. Ideally, the realization of those qualities will put a premium stamp on the quality of service you bring to the organization. Companies place the weight of candidate selection onto the shoulders of the Human Resources department. Recruiters have a difficult job. They must select from a pool of candidates with great optimism, selecting the best person with the greatest skills and experience (what I refer to as your **product**) resulting in the most benefit to their organization (the way you perform is your **service**), better known as the differentiators of "your business".

It can be quite difficult to be an effective leader if you are not aware of your true potential, emotional maturity, brand of self-discipline and standards for excellence. Seeking buy-in or articulating goals and visions for other people goes much more smoothly when you've practiced that skill effectively enough to take care of your own aspirations and needs. People of all levels in their professional journey are successful to the degree they can articulate what they aspire to be (vision), are committed to self-discovery and execute a plan for achievement. When people are truly focused and engaged, they become CEO's of their destiny. Many people want greater success but do not realize that through their potential they have the POWER to do something about it. When someone says you have lots of potential, they are acknowledging your natural ability to excel at something. However, it must be fueled by self-evaluation and a vision that gives you the freedom to choose your direction to a destination designed by you and for you. Not one that is designed by others. Your Mission is POSSIBLE!

This book will help you access inner-strength and value, then guide you step-by-step on how to execute a course of action to achieve EXTRAORDINARY results in your career and life. By the end of the week, with *POWER Your Potential BOOST CAMP® Leadership Edition: 7 Days to Professional Success and Satisfaction,* you'll have a highly personalized implementation plan that you can follow to map out and achieve the career of your dreams. The talent is already inside you—all you need is a seven-day BOOST.

Day 1: Discover Your True Potential

Day 2: Enlarge Your Vision

Day 3: Renovate Your Belief System

Day 4: Set S.M.A.R.T. POWER Goals

Day 5: Build Your Dream Network

Day 6: Take Care of Your Greatest Asset (YOU!)

Day 7: Create Your Action Plan

As the true leader in you emerges, continue to invest in your personal and professional development, value education, take stock in networking, health and diversity, while keeping a pulse on your vision. By doing the steps outlined in *POWER Your Potential BOOST CAMP®* Leadership Edition: *7 Days to Professional Success and Satisfaction,* you will gain a strong professional foundation upon which success can be built. Combined, these efforts will give you a BOOST for taking your possibilities for Enhancing Your POWER to THRIVE to new heights. Flip the page and let's get started!

Day 1

Discover your true potential

"Circumstances may cause interruptions and delays, but never lose sight of your goal. Prepare yourself in every way you can by increasing your knowledge and adding to your experience, so that you can make the most of your opportunity when it occurs..."

-Mario Andretti

Day 1

Discover Your True Potential

Potential is described by most as the **POWER**, strength, and possibilities associated with the use of your natural abilities. When someone tells you that you have "lots of potential," they are acknowledging your natural ability to excel and that you have many possibilities of becoming an achiever of great things. The first step in the ***POWER** Your Potential BOOST CAMP* is to clearly identify your professional potential. This is the time to look deep within yourself and dream **BIG**.

You will know you are reaching your full professional potential when you are engaging in professional activities that you enjoy and complete extremely well, and you are living a life that really fits your true self. When you begin working toward everything you want to achieve at the end of this week you will actively be igniting the **POWER** of your leadership potential.

STEP 1: IDENTIFY YOUR EXISTING STRENGTHS AND SKILLS

Pulling together and acknowledging your positive qualities and skills is the first step toward **POWERing** your potential. You have great talents, abilities and skills that, if put to use and developed, will make greater possibilities available to you. Everyone has potential, whether or not they know what their true potential is. By taking an in-depth journey of self-discovery, you will find that the answer to the question, "What is my potential?" is already inside of you. The first step to answering this question is to identify your existing skills. Knowing all the skills you already possess will help you decide on a career path or help you determine which skills you will need to develop in order to pursue the career of your dreams. Just remember these are not tests, they are tools. The more information you have about yourself, the closer you will be to knowing what steps you need to take to **POWER** your leadership potential. Rather than taking your talents for granted, be grateful for your gifts and use them.

Give Yourself a BOOST: Completing a Leadership BOOST Analysis

If there were no restriction, what would be the ideal career for you? Based on your current strengths, what could be possible for you? Could any of your weaknesses seriously threaten your career or business? If so, how can you overcome those vulnerabilities to ensure your success? These are some of the questions that the Leadership **B.O.O.S.T.** analysis can help you answer.

A Leadership **B.O.O.S.T.** analysis allows you to identify the professional Benefits, Opportunities, Obstacles, Strengths, and Threats of making a change towards enhancing your **POWER** to THRIVE.

Benefits (positive things that could come from change)
Opportunities (external supports for change)
Obstacles (external challenges around change)
Strengths (internal supports for change)
Threats (internal challenges around change)

You can use the results of the Leadership **B.O.O.S.T.** analysis to identify which steps will help you acquire the skills you need to achieve your full professional potential. You can also use the results to focus your efforts in areas where you are strong and where the greatest opportunities lie in your current or new career.

The Leadership **B.O.O.S.T.** analysis is very useful in identifying your personal potential and the effective ways to use what is revealed in your responses to promote yourself. To give you a jumpstart, the following is a list of sample Benefits, Opportunities, Obstacles, Strengths and Threats. Of course, this list is a tool to help start your thinking process. Some items might apply to you; many may not, and there are a myriad of additional possibilities for each category. Remember that what is a strength and what is a threat are totally subjective and depend on your chosen profession and your personal desires. If you want to be a vice president of Human Resources, it is a threat if you are not great at communicating policies or giving positive and high-quality feedback. For the same job, though, not being good at preparing a balance sheet probably will not be a threat that really matters. If you are going to be a software developer who mainly works alone and is not expected to be the best communicator, then not working well in large groups perhaps will not be a threat you need to worry about. If you already know what you want to do, you can choose the strengths and threats that apply directly to your desired profession. If you are still in the process of discovery about what you want to be, then considering a few options below might be more helpful for you.

In each of the following subsections, circle or highlight the statements that resonate with you most:

Sample Benefits (positive things that could come from change):

- Pride in a job well done.
- Interest in new tasks or responsibilities (professional growth).
- Genuine excitement about the work I am doing.
- More energy and time for self, family and friends.

- Better salary, more financial stability.
- Better health benefits or retirement security.
- More personal satisfaction.
- More supportive working conditions/environment.
- Less commuting time.

Sample Opportunities (external supports for change):

- There is a promotion coming up in my company.
- I know someone who can help me get an interview in the department or at the company where I want to work.
- There is a degree program in my field at a local college.
- I have a very supportive boss who wants to help me succeed.
- I have a great mentor who can introduce me to contacts in my desired field.
- I can use the alumnae network of my school(s) to make connections.
- My job offers flextime so I can take classes while working.
- My employer reimburses educational expenses for degrees in my field.
- There is an upcoming job fair I can attend to meet potential employers.
- There is a union or professional organization in my field that I can join for resources and support.
- There are books I can read to help me learn more about my field.
- There are internships I can seek to gain experience in a new field.
- I have a good friend or a supportive partner who can help take care of my children while I work toward my goals.
- I have some money saved to support me while I go to school or build my experience in a new field.
- I can hire someone to help me achieve and improve in

areas that I know are not my strengths.

- There are people I can ask to help me achieve my goals.
- One of my connections (former classmates, co-workers, supervisors, friends, acquaintances) has a position at a new company or organization.
- I have recently received some extra income (bonus, inheritance) that has allowed a window for greater risk taking.
- A class or educational program is starting in my field.
- There are upcoming openings in my company for promotions.
- I have extra vacation days that I can use for professional training/conferences in my field.

Sample Obstacles (external challenges around change):

- The economy is weak right now.
- The companies in my field are generally downsizing.
- There are not a lot of positions for what I want to do.
- My desired field is extremely competitive.
- My boss/coworker is not supportive of my goals.
- My partner/friends/family are not supportive of my leadership goals.
- The technology changes so quickly I am not sure how to keep up.
- The career I want may not pay well enough to support my needs.
- I need a degree to work in my desired field.
- I need certain experience/skills to get a promotion.

Sample Strengths (internal supports for change):

- I am easy to get along with.
- I have a solid education in my desired field.
- I am enthusiastic and dedicated.

- I am supportive of my co-worker's success.
- I get a lot done without supervision.
- I have a good memory.
- I am a good listener.
- I am physically fit for the job.
- I can come up with creative solutions to problems.
- I am calm under pressure.
- I treat others with respect.
- I have strong verbal skills.
- I have strong writing skills.
- I have strong mathematical skills.
- I am good with my hands.
- I can fix anything.
- I love a challenge.
- I am flexible and I can roll with the punches.
- I am always on time.
- I meet my deadlines.
- I keep on top of things.
- I can keep track of many details at once.
- I have a good sense of humor.
- I have a pleasant voice.
- I have a professional appearance.
- I am an inspiring leader.
- I work well with others.
- I am a fast learner.
- I am thorough and I take pride in a job well done.
- I am supportive of the people I work with.
- I am good with dates and scheduling.
- I am good at looking at the big picture.
- I am good at completing specific defined tasks.
- I have a good attention span and enjoy focusing my attention.
- I have stamina for long-term projects.

Sample Threats (internal challenges around change) to overcome to THRIVE:

- I tend to be moody or grouchy with others.
- I have not yet gotten the education or degree I need.
- I lose interest easily.
- I tend to be so competitive that I do not work well with co-workers.
- I need close supervision to stay on track.
- I have a hard time remembering details and I rarely write things down.
- I tend to be disorganized.
- I have physical limitations that could interfere with my job.
- I do not do well under pressure.
- I can sometimes be confrontational and lose my temper.
- I find it difficult to find the right words for what I want to say.
- I do not feel confident about my writing skills.
- I prefer to do a job I can master and be comfortable with, rather than one that will challenge me.
- I am not very resourceful or good with book skills.
- I do not feel confident working with numbers.
- It upsets me when things change all the time.
- I am often late or I forget to show up altogether.
- I often fall behind or miss my deadlines.
- I tend to procrastinate.
- I do not do well when asked to do many things at once.
- I tend to be a bit sloppy in my appearance.
- I am not good at inspiring others to work for me.
- I do not like telling others what to do.
- It is hard for me to keep track of dates and times.
- It is hard for me to keep the big picture in mind.
- I have a short attention span and get bored if things stay the same for too long.
- I get tired or frustrated easily with long-term projects.

Now that you are getting the idea, it is almost time to complete your own Leadership **B.O.O.S.T.** Analysis. The following is a sample analysis of an employee who hopes to be promoted in the next year or two.

Sample Personalized Leadership BOOST Analysis

Benefits: *More satisfying/interesting job, better pay, professional satisfaction, BOOST in self-esteem.*

Opportunities: *I could sign up for optional technology training workshop offered by my company; my boss said she is open to supporting my professional growth, so I could also volunteer to do preliminary research for new projects, with the hope of gaining additional experience that could lead to a management position.*

Obstacles: *There are several of my co-workers who are also seeking promotions, some of whom have more education than I.*

Strengths: *I am good at communication and thus I am willing to ask the boss what specific steps I might take to give me an edge with future promotions. I am also a hard worker who is willing to put in extra time and effort to get the job I really want.*

Threats: *I tend to get intimidated when I am in competition with others and give up easily. (I may need to enlist an outside accountability partner/ support person to make sure I continue putting myself out there each week, rather than letting myself fade into the background.)*

Now complete your own Leadership B.O.O.S.T. analysis. You will be able to use the answers in later exercises. For now, just explore, and do not worry about solutions.

Your Personalized Leadership BOOST Analysis

Benefits:

_____

_____

_____

_____

Opportunities:

_____

_____

_____

_____

Obstacles:

_____

_____

_____

_____

Strengths:

_____

_____

_____

_____

Threats:

_____

_____

_____

_____

Identifying Your Transferable Skills

Many career seekers have a variety of job experiences and job titles that do not necessarily relate to the types of positions they would like to be hired for or promoted into. For that reason, it is extremely important that you learn to identify transferable skills that market you as a well-rounded, highly qualified employee. A transferable skills inventory will help you determine what you are good at and what you really enjoy doing. In identifying your transferable skills, remember not to overlook the skills you have gained from everyday living, for example:

☐ Displaying endurance under pressure

☐ Describing feelings and needs

☐ Financial planning

☐ Influencing others

☐ Coming up with creative solutions to problems

☐ Thinking out of the box

☐ Keeping your focus on positive results

☐ Taking risks

☐ Handling details

☐ Comforting or inspiring others

Use the transferable skills exercise on the following pages to help you identify at least ten of your transferable skills, and then you will learn how to transform that list into transferable skills statements. To help you get started, review the following lists of transferable skills and check all the skills you possess. They are divided into five broad areas and then are divided into more specific job skills.

Communication: *the skillful expression, transmission and interpretation of knowledge and ideas.*

- ☐ Speaking effectively
- ☐ Writing concisely
- ☐ Listening attentively
- ☐ Expressing ideas
- ☐ Facilitating group discussion
- ☐ Providing appropriate feedback
- ☐ Negotiating
- ☐ Perceiving nonverbal messages
- ☐ Persuading
- ☐ Reporting information
- ☐ Interviewing
- ☐ Editing

Research and Planning: *the search for specific knowledge and the ability to conceptualize future needs and solutions for meeting those needs.*

- ☐ Forecasting and predicting
- ☐ Brainstorming ideas
- ☐ Identifying problems
- ☐ Imagining alternatives
- ☐ Identifying resources
- ☐ Gathering information

- [ ] Solving problems
- [ ] Setting goals
- [ ] Extracting important information
- [ ] Defining needs
- [ ] Analyzing
- [ ] Developing evaluation strategies

Human Relations: *the use of interpersonal skills for resolving conflict, relating well with people, and helping others.*

- [ ] Developing rapport
- [ ] Being sensitive
- [ ] Listening
- [ ] Conveying feelings
- [ ] Providing support for others
- [ ] Motivating
- [ ] Sharing credit
- [ ] Counseling and mediating
- [ ] Cooperating
- [ ] Delegating with respect
- [ ] Representing others
- [ ] Perceiving feelings and situations
- [ ] Asserting

Organization, Management and Leadership: *the ability to supervise, direct and guide individuals or groups in the completion of tasks and fulfillment of goals.*

☐ Initiating new ideas

☐ Coordinating tasks

☐ Managing groups

☐ Planning and executing strategies

☐ Communicating the mission

☐ Delegating the responsibility

☐ Creating inclusion strategies

☐ Coaching

☐ **EnPOWERing** others

☐ Counseling

☐ Inspiring a shared vision

☐ Promoting change

☐ Selling ideas or products

☐ Making decisions with others

☐ Managing conflict

Work Survival: *the day-to-day skills that assist in promoting effective production and work satisfaction.*

☐ Implementing decisions

☐ Cooperating

☐   Enforcing policies

☐   Attending to detail

☐   Meeting goals

☐   Working as part of a team

☐   Enlisting help

☐   Accepting responsibility

☐   Setting and meeting deadlines

☐   Organizing

☐   Making decisions

☐   Being punctual

☐   Managing time

Give Yourself a BOOST: Complete a Transferable Skills Inventory

To help you determine your full range of transferable skills, complete a separate version of the Transferable Skills Inventory Worksheet for each on campus leadership role, volunteer position and job you have had and each related activity you have participated in using the following guidelines:

1. In the **Tasks** column list each function of your job or activity.
2. In the **Skills** column list the specific skills you use or used to complete the corresponding task in the first column. Use the examples of tangible skills listed above. Do not limit yourself to the ones listed.
3. In the **Skill Level** column rate yourself according to your level of competency (1=highly skilled; 2=moderately skilled; 3=basic skills).

16

4. In the **Enjoy** column place a check next to those skills
    that you enjoy using.

Transferable Skills Inventory Worksheet			
Job or Activity #1:			
Tasks	Skills	Skill Level	Enjoy?

Transferable Skills Inventory Worksheet			
Job or Activity #2:			
Tasks	Skills	Skill Level	Enjoy?

Transferable Skills Inventory Worksheet			
Job or Activity #3:			
Tasks	Skills	Skill Level	Enjoy?

Give Yourself a BOOST: Writing Your Transferable Skills Statement

Once you have identified your transferable skills, develop them into statements you can use in a cover letter, at an interview, or an employee evaluation to show employers exactly why you are the best person for the job. Below are sample statements about transferable skills. Each is followed by an example and a connection to a specific job.

Sample transferable skill: Speaking effectively

Sample transferable skill statement: I have extensive experience communicating with classmates, co-workers and clients. In my role as director of operations, I was responsible for presenting organizational changes in a series of successful companywide meetings.

Sample transferable skill: Identifying problems

Sample transferable skill statement: As the president of the Student Government Association (SGA) at my university, I held weekly meetings to support students and also identify potential problems before they became major issues on campus.

Sample transferable skill: Being sensitive

Sample transferable skill statement: As a team player I have shown empathy and offered support to my co-workers, which minimized team silos increased member participation and inclusion, and my department's morale and productivity during challenging projects.

Sample transferable skill: Coordinating tasks

Sample transferable skill statement: I am an extremely organized person, and I successfully apply these skills to coordinating the tasks of employees under my supervision.

Sample transferable skill: Financial Planner

Sample transferable skill statement: As a full-time homemaker I handled the household budget for ten years. In addition to paying household expenses without ever bouncing a check or failing to pay a bill on time, I also developed a successful savings and retirement investment plan for many family members and friends.

Using the skills you have identified on your transferable skills worksheets and the job you want to have, write five transferable skill statements. As much as possible, *choose from the skills you are already using and/ or excel at.* That way you will be more likely to seek out a career or job where you will enjoy much success and look forward to going to work each day.

Transferable skill #1:

Transferable skill statement (Review the examples again if you get stuck):

_____

_____

_____

_____

_____

Transferable skill #2:

_____

Transferable skill statement:

_____

_____

_____

_____

_____

Transferable skill #3:

_____

Transferable skill statement:

_____

_____

_____

_____

_____

Transferable skill #4:

_____

Transferable skill statement:

_____

_____

_____

_____

_____

Transferable skill #5:

_____

Transferable skill statement:

_____

_____

_____

_____

_____

Congratulations! Now that you have identified your skills and taken the time to articulate these skills in statements, you are well prepared to quickly and efficiently write effective cover letters. You can also review these skills and statements before networking events and job interviews so that all your skills are at the front of your mind.

Give Yourself a BOOST: Keeping Track of the Skills You Want to Build

While it is important to emphasize your best skills to others, you should not forget about the skills you want to improve. Go through your transferable skills worksheets again, and this time note any skills that you enjoy using, but which you rated yourself a 2 (moderate skill level) or 3 (basic skill level). Also note any skills on which you rated yourself low but are crucial to your success. List them here, and you will come back to them later, when you get to the chapter on building **S.M.A.R.T.** goals.

_____

_____

_____

_____

_____

STEP 2: DESCRIBE YOUR BEST QUALITIES

While skills are external talents you develop with experience and guidance, qualities are internal tendencies and conditions that make you unique. Identifying and communicating your best qualities is another way to set yourself apart and enhance your chances of getting a job that really fits your most authentic self. If you are short on experience and skills, emphasizing your best qualities is an essential way to amp up your chances for advancement or of getting the job you want.

The following is a list of positive qualities to get you started in identifying your own positive qualities. **Circle or highlight the box next to the qualities that describe you most.**

      ☐   Optimism (a tendency to expect the best or focus on the positive)

      ☐   Passion (enthusiasm for pursuing your dreams)

      ☐   Confidence (a feeling of assurance in your talents and skills)

☐ Intuition (an ability to sense what will work best in any given situation)

☐ Vision (seeing how things could be, rather than being limited by how things are)

☐ Enthusiasm (energy for and a positive attitude around pursuing your goals and dreams, while challenging others to do the same)

☐ Commitment (consistently pursuing your goals, even after setbacks)

☐ Connection (maintaining relationships with people who share your vision and goals and coach others on how it is done)

☐ Resourcefulness (an ability to seek out the skills and support and whatever else you need to ensure your success and those of others)

☐ Creativity (an originality of vision, a unique expressiveness and an inventive approach)

☐ Ambition (a willingness to seize opportunities and create your own whenever possible)

☐ Self-awareness (an understanding of who you are, what you stand for, and what motivates you to take action)

☐ Self-supportiveness (a dedication to spending time on introspection and self-discovery, such as what you really think and feel-if you are reading this book and giving your all to these exercises, check this one!)

☐ Proactive (a willingness to take responsibility and action for your own happiness and success)

☐ Perseverance (an ability to spin challenges into your greatest motivators-and sometimes biggest advantages)

☐ Independence (a willingness to take control and ownership of your life and never let go)

☐ Courage (an ability to take risks and make yourself vulnerable)

☐ _____

☐ _____

☐ _____

☐ _____

☐ _____

☐ _____

Give Yourself a BOOST: Promote Your Best Qualities

Your professional success could come down to a little bit of self-promotion! To promote your best qualities, choose two to four of the qualities you have selected from the above list (or other qualities that you possess and would like to capitalize on in your professional life). Describe these qualities in the form of statements you can share with potential or existing employers. Describe your best qualities as if you were a telemarketer selling a product, including examples from your own experiences that support your statements. Also, state the connection between each quality and the job you want.

Here are a few examples to **help** get you started:

Sample Quality #1: *Confidence*

Sample Quality Statement: *I handle all tasks with effectiveness and speed*

Sample Quality #2: *An understanding of what motivates me*

Sample Quality Statement: *I work best in a collaborative and supportive environment in which I am able to exchange ideas freely to come up with optimal solutions.*

Sample Quality #3: *A refusal to let other people dictate to me how I should live*

Sample Quality Statement: *I have a clear vision of what I would like to accomplish in this position, and I welcome the opportunity to share my ideas with you.*

Sample Quality #4: *A willingness to take control and ownership of your life*

Sample Quality Statement: *I work well independently and as part of a team. If given the opportunity, I will be a creative asset to your company*

Refer to the examples again if you get stuck.

Quality #1:

_____

Quality Statement (if possible, include a specific example of how this quality has helped you professionally and its connection to the job you are seeking); Refer back to the examples again if you get stuck:

_____

_____

_____

_____

Quality #2:

Quality Statement (if possible, include a specific example of how this quality has helped you professionally and its connection to the job you are seeking).

_____

_____

_____

_____

Quality #3:

_____

Quality Statement (if possible, include a specific example of how this quality has helped you professionally and its connection to the job you are seeking).

_____

_____

_____

_____

Quality #4:

_____

Quality Statement (if possible, include a specific example of how this quality has helped you professionally and its connection to the job you are seeking).

_____

_____

STEP 3: SHOW THAT YOU'RE A S.T.A.R.

Often during interviews, social events, or meetings, you will get the opportunity to highlight your unique talents. A very effective way to do it is to introduce career success stories about how you overcame significant challenges. You may have suggested a creative solution to handle an employee performance problem. Maybe you instituted a step-by-step process to reduce customer complaints. Perhaps your persistence paid off to close a multiyear contract with the largest customer the company has ever seen.

Challenges serve as a test of your commitment and endurance. The **S.T.A.R.** system (Situation, Task, Action, Result) is a simple but effective way of promoting your skills and talents by documenting success stories around your strengths that you can share at appropriate moments and opportunities. A **S.T.A.R.** story includes the following:

- **Situation:** What was the job/circumstance?
- **Task:** What problem or challenge did the situation present?
- **Action:** What specific steps did you take to address the task at hand?
- **Result:** What was the positive outcome of your action?

The following are two examples of **S.T.A.R.** stories used in varying situations.

S.T.A.R. sample #1: *Using a social situation to advance a job opportunity* Question at a party: "Oh, I did not realize you worked in sales. We are looking for a new salesperson in our department. What have you done professionally?"

- **Situation:** I am very interested in learning more about the sales position in your department.
- **Task:** In my current role as a regional director of sales, I have been in charge of launching the expansion of our training curriculum and services.
- **Action:** Immediately after the launch, I started contacting major corporations in the Atlanta, Georgia, area to introduce them to our mobile leadership training and compliance programs. In the past year I have built relationships with the majority of them, and more than a third of them, have either called me for more information or have registered their groups for one or more sessions.
- **Result:** Because of my strong reputation with previous clients and in the industry, I have successfully closed fifty nine percent of all accounts contacted and I have consistently ranked among the top five salespeople in my company.

S.T.A.R. sample #1: Sharing a S.T.A.R. story in a yearly on-the-job work evaluation meeting

- **Situation:** Create a format for achieving higher service compliance ratings in the southwestern region.
- **Task:** The goal was to put adequate procedures in place to ensure the largest return on investment for first-time foreclosure buyers.
- **Action:** I developed and implemented a system for assessing market performance and monitoring the feedback from our customers. I consistently reviewed customer service feedback and developed strategies to improve service based on customer responses. I was proactive in identifying and meeting customer needs; collaborating with them to solve their problems; tracking the frequency of complaints as a way to assess performance, developing and maintaining trust, and

maintaining constructive relationships during and after the improvement phase.

- **Result:** Our customer satisfaction rating increased by 39% over the previous year and repeat business nearly doubled in less than one year.

Give Yourself a BOOST: Make Yourself a S.T.A.R. Achiever

It is time to start building an archive of your own **S.T.A.R.** stories. On the lines provided below, document four of your most current or impressive success stories. Choose situations that highlight your best skills, strengths, and qualities or your best use of decision-making skills. Ideally, you will write at least one **S.T.A.R.** story for each of your major professional accomplishments, so that when the opportunity arises to share these stories, you will be prepared.

Using the **S.T.A.R.** system, describe a workplace or personal *situation* that you are extremely proud of. Include the *task* that needed to be accomplished, the *action(s)* you took to accomplish the task, and the positive *result* of that action. As you choose which situations to feature, it is ideal to use a difficult situation that you resolved effectively. **Refer to the examples again if you get stuck.**

S.T.A.R. Story #1:

_____

Situation:

_____

_____

_____

_____

_____

Task:

_____

_____

_____

_____

_____

Action:

_____

_____

_____

_____

_____

Result:

_____

_____

_____

_____

_____

S.T.A.R. Story #2:

_____

Situation:

_____

_____

_____

_____

_____

Task:

_____

_____

_____

_____

Action:

_____

_____

_____

_____

Result:

_____

_____

_____

_____

S.T.A.R. Story #3:

_____

Situation:

_____

_____

_____

_____

_____

Task:

_____

_____

_____

_____

Action:

_____

_____

_____

_____

Result:

_____

_____

_____

_____

Save and remember these stories. They can be very valuable when you are being considered for promotions, doing interviews, and building your network of referrals. If you feel awkward making yourself a **S.T.A.R.,** remember the words of productivity coach and author Lee Milteer: *"Success is an inside job."*

Most people are six inches away from greatness-that is the space between your ears (your brain). Storing these stories in your brain allows you to bring them forward when you need them most. The repetition will allow you to become more comfortable about vocalizing your accomplishment. A good number of professional opportunities come up unexpectedly, when you do not have time to stop and prepare. Already having done this work ensures that you are prepared for all the opportunities that come your way.

Day 2

Enlarge Your Vision

*"You must first envision the impossible before achieving the unbelievable... **Your Mission is Possible!**"*

-Dr. Valerie D.W. James

Day 2

Enlarge Your Vision

Where do you see yourself in the future? Wherever it is, that is where you are most likely to end up. If you imagine yourself thriving in a career you love, that pays you well, that you are great at, that is where you are headed. Your mind is a **POWERful** creative force. Your perception of your place in the world greatly determines your reality.

If you imagine yourself going nowhere or never getting to do what you really love, then you will not be inspired to take positive action. When you regularly picture exactly what it is you want to achieve, you will make decisions to support that end result.

Think about it this way: If you keep seeing yourself getting rejected for a promotion or from the jobs you want, how will you feel about spending the day reworking your resume or taking a class to advance your skills? You will probably feel defeated and think, "Why should I bother with it? It is not going to work out, so I might as well just watch TV." Allow yourself to enlarge your vision and picture yourself achieving your ultimate career goal, and you will feel hopeful and enthusiastic. If you imagine that everyone who reads that new resume is going to be really excited to meet you, you will want to jump right on it, revisit it, update it, and upgrade it. Your upgraded resume will make you way more likely to get that dream job-especially if you promise yourself that nothing is going to stop you and that you are just going to keep building your skills and experience until you get that dream job. Remember: the only way to fail is to give up! As long as you keep trying, you are fail-proof!

Give Yourself a BOOST: Envisioning Success

There are patterns for success and for failure. Success often leaves signs. People who have succeed are not successful by chance; people who succeed regularly do things to make themselves feel good and feeling good motivates them to take continuous action toward their vision of success.

Write what your ideal professional success will look like:

_____

_____

_____

Note what experiences and people in your life have inspired this vision of success:

_____

_____

_____

Write a list of people you think are successful. What is it about them that makes them a success in your eyes?

_____

_____

_____

If you could modify your current vision of success in any way, what would you change?

_____

_____

_____

Now make a list of people who are successful based on your expanded definition of success.

Give Yourself a BOOST: Dream Big

Here is your chance to dream big and come up with the specifics of your dream career. If any negative thoughts come up like "Why bother? I know I will never get what I want anyway" or any other negative thoughts tell yourself you are going to listen to and address those fears and negative beliefs tomorrow, while you are working through the next chapter. For now, tell your inner skeptic that this is just imaginative playtime.

Answer the following questions based on *your ideal dream world*. **Do** not put down anything that merely feels "good enough" or that you think will please other people. Do not modify your dream to make it feel more realistic or attainable. Just envision that you are going to be granted the opportunity to be promoted into or have the perfect job or business. This exercise is your preparation to ensure that you do not believe for anything less than your version of excellence. Let's get started!

What skills and talents will you use (you may want to refer to the Transferable Skills Inventory Worksheet from day 1, especially noting the skills you enjoy using):

_____

_____

_____

What will your ideal work environment and circumstances be like (check all that apply):

☐ My workplace will be fast-paced and exciting.

☐ My workplace will be calm and predictable.

☐ I will work alone or with just a few co-workers.

☐ I will work with many co-workers or for a big company.

☐ I will work for a high profile, well-known company.

☐ I will start my own business.

☐ I will work 9 to 5.

☐ I will work evenings or nights.

☐ I will work part-time.

☐ I will work at my own pace. I will work someplace with childcare.

☐ I will be my own boss or have a lot of responsibilities.

☐ I will have a supportive boss but not too many responsibilities.

☐ I will work from home.

☐ I will work someplace that is near my home.

☐ My job will involve relocating.

☐ My job will feel meaningful.

☐ My job will feel valued.

☐ My job will be prestigious and impress others.

☐ My job will help others.

☐ My job will help change the world for the better.

☐ My job will financially support my family and me.

To be successful you have to be self-driven. If you are doing something you are genuinely excited about and have a positive work/life balance, when your eyes open in the morning you will feel motivated to get up, not hit the snooze button. When you expect happiness and adapt a positive lifestyle, you will be happy and content with who you are. With that in mind, *plan out what your prefect workday would look like.* What would make you want to get out of bed in the morning? (Do not forget to include amusing things, time to take care of yourself, time for family and friends and plenty of rest):

5 A.M.

_____

6 A.M.

_____

7 A.M.

_____

8 A.M.

_____

9 A.M.

_____

10 A.M.

_____

11 A.M.

_____

NOON

_____

1 P.M.

_____

2 P.M.

_____

3 P.M.

_____

4 P.M.

_____

5 P.M.

_____

6 P.M.

_____

7 P.M.

_____

8 P.M.

_____

9 P.M.

_____

10 P.M.

_____

11 P.M.

_____

MIDNIGHT

_____

1 A.M.

_____

2 A.M.

_____

3 A.M.

_____

4 A.M.

_____

Describe your dream job, in your own words:

_____

_____

_____

_____

_____

Give Yourself a BOOST: Picturing Your Dream

The clearer you can picture something, the more likely it will become a reality. On a separate sheet of paper, using paints, crayons, colored pencils, or whatever sparks your imagination, draw a picture of yourself in your ideal career. If you hate to draw, cut out pictures from magazines or print out images off the Internet and paste them into a collage. Give yourself at least an hour to make something that truly represents your dream. When you are finished, frame it and hang it somewhere you will see it every day. Here is a sample of my vision boards.

Remember: *"You must first envision the impossible before achieving the unbelievable"*. Your **Mission Is Possible** too!

THE POWER OF VISUALIZATION

Visualization is a **POWERful** strategy for achieving future goals and visualization is even more **POWERful** when coupled with putting the image on paper. Ultimately, in life we move toward the reality we see in our minds.

I recently heard an interesting story about a young boy in the Midwest who attended a one-room school some decades ago. Please allow me to paraphrase the story, one day his teacher was speaking on the subject of imagination. To bring this subject to life for the students, the teacher instructed the class to draw a picture of a flower. As they drew, the teacher walked around the room looking at the images the students were drawing. When she got to one little boy's desk she looked at his paper and noticed that he had drawn faces on his flowers. This is my self-made image of his flower.

Example of a flower with a happy face

The teacher said, "Flowers do not have faces, silly." His reply was, "Mine do." The little boy was Walt Disney; he had a vision, of bringing the impossible to life. He never lost sight of the vision for making the world a happier place for everyone. As a result, he became one of the richest and most famous personalities in the world.

Another great example of the **POWER** of visualization is the story of Tara Holland. She dreamed of becoming Miss America. In 1994 she entered the Miss Florida pageant and won the title of first runner-up. She did the same thing for three years straight, and then in 1997 she entered the Miss Kansas pageant and won the title. That same year she was crowned Miss America and her dream came true. When a reporter asked her if she was nervous, she responded "no" because she had walked down that runway thousands of times before in her mind's eye. By continuously envisioning her dream, she fueled her efforts until they eventually led to the success she desired.

Give Yourself a BOOST: Visualize Your Dream

Spending five to ten minutes each day visualizing yourself being successful in your dream career will fuel you as you take all the necessary steps to get there. All you have to do is get into a comfortable position, close your eyes, and watch a "movie" in your imagination. See yourself dressed in the clothes you would wear. Picture your surroundings in detail, allowing yourself to see, hear, and feel the details of your dream workplace. Watch yourself performing the tasks of your job with great enthusiasm and skill. Imagine others praising your efforts, telling you how much they admire your talents. Feel how your body feels when receiving all this praise. Think, "I am doing a great job, and I feel proud of my skills and accomplishments. There is no job I would rather do." Feel all the good physical sensations that arise from positive visualization and allow your body to enjoy a taste of your dream job. That feeling is great. RIGHT! Soon, you will be there.

Just keep taking the next step and the next step until visualization becomes your reality.

To make your dream for ultimate success and satisfaction become a reality, get a small "things to do board" and place it on your desk, at the office, or even on your home wall near the door, and every morning commit to writing one thing you can do that day to bring you closer to your dream. At the end of the day, on your way home, or when you are winding down for the day, jot down or make a mental note of at least one thing you did that moved you closer to making your dream come true.

The following are some examples:

- Speak to my manager about the open position I am interested in
- Updated my resume to include my most recent promotion, expanded responsibilities and accomplishments
- Jogged forty-five minutes a day
- Drank two bottles of water
- Organized your business files
- Introduced myself to seven new business prospects
- Reviewed previously worked steps in the **POWER Your Potential BOOST CAMP** book to master my game plan for success

Day 3

Renovate Your Belief System

"Whether You Think You Can Or You Can't... You're Right!"
-Henry Ford

Day 3

Renovate Your Belief System

Now that you have a clearer vision of your dream career, it is time to identify and address any defeating or negative beliefs you have around your ability to reach your professional potential. There will likely be some obstacles to overcome as you work your way toward reaching your potential but you never want to be the obstacle that is getting in your own way!

In the past, you may have shot down your own dreams by saying things like this:

- I cannot see myself being successful.
- That will never happen for me.
- I just prepare for the worst and hope for the best. Whatever happens, happens.
- There is nothing I can do about it.
- This is just my lot in life.
- I am not **POWERful** enough.
- That is how life goes. At least that is how *my* life goes.

Maybe when asked what you see in your future, you have allowed, "I do not know" to serve as your answer. If so, you are certainly not alone. Sometimes, to protect ourselves from the fears and risks of going for what we really want in life, we tell

51

ourselves negative things about our potential, or we simply do not allow ourselves to imagine what we could accomplish if we **POWERed** our potential. It is not because we do not want to succeed, but rather because on some level we are trying to protect ourselves from the pain of rejection, failure and disappointment. We try to convince ourselves in advance that we can never have what we want, so we will not feel upset if we do not get it.

It is a caring impulse; we are trying to protect ourselves from pain, yet it is also a limiting habit. It is time to reassure yourself consciously that you can handle the painful feelings that come from setbacks; because you're making a promise to yourself that you're not going to fail-because you are not going to give up. You are going to keep taking steps forward-sometimes baby steps, sometimes giant leaps-until you reach the career success you desire.

It is time to transform these negative beliefs and take a chance on you. *The **POWER** Your Potential BOOST CAMP* will help you develop positive beliefs, crucial support network focus that you need, to weather setbacks.

Just remember: unless you give up, there is no such thing as failure, only temporary obstacles and setbacks. By offering yourself comfort and encouragement when faced with obstacles, you will transform any setback into a mere pit stop on your journey to achieving greater avenues for success and satisfaction.

Admitting what we want can be terrifying: What if I fail? What if I find out I am not good enough? What will people think? How could I live with the humiliation?

The truth is, plenty of successful people face these kinds of self-doubts. But rather than giving up because of them, they keep believing their dreams are possible. They reassure themselves and then *dream BIGGER*. Each and every person on this planet has great potential and a wellspring of inner **POWER** from which they can draw.

When you have a career that allows you to express your natural gifts, talents, and best qualities, you will have discovered your ultimate professional purpose. You will find that your work inspires you, nourishes you, and gives you energy.

If your dream career seems a million miles away, do not worry. It really doesn't matter where you are in your life right now. Change occurs second by second. Whether you are almost there or you have a long way to go, you will be able to reach your true potential. Just hold your head to the sky, keep going, and take things one step at a time.

CHOOSE YOUR WORDS CAREFULLY

The words you speak and the words you choose are very important to maintaining an optimistic perspective. Positive self-talk reduces anxiety and elicit positive outcomes.

For example, consider the word "do not." If you call out to a child, "Do not slam the refrigerator door!" what is the next sound you will probably hear? Barn! The majority of that message came through: "Slam the refrigerator door!" But the most important words, "do not," got lost in the delivery of that message.

If you phrase your statements in terms of the positive, then even if a few words get lost, you will still get a positive result. If you say, "Close the door slowly," the child will be much more likely to comply. Likewise, if you tell yourself, "Do not give up," it will not be nearly as effective as if you keep telling yourself, "Keep going, be strong! You can do it!"

Another dangerous word is "can't." People often say I *can't* go back to school, I *can't* ask for that favor, or I *can't* remember names at networking events. The more we say, "can't," the more "can't" becomes our reality. If you catch yourself saying you can't do something, turn it around into something more positive: "I want to get the skills I need," "I would like to go back to school," or "I must come up with a creative solution to help me remember names," are all more likely to gain the positive results you want. Allow yourself to move past the negative "can't" programming that creates false limitations. Do not let this word rob you of your true potential.

Give Yourself a BOOST: Say Something Positive

Repeat after me:

- I am destined for greatness.
- I am a winner.
- I can do this.
- It is all about me right now.
- I am blessed.
- I have the ability and **POWER** to realize and actualize my dreams.
- I am **POWERful.**
- I must first envision the impossible before I can achieve the unbelievable.
- My mission is possible!

You have just made some bold statements confirming your goal of achieving your professional potential. Post these phrases in a place where you can see them and recite them every day. Put them on your refrigerator, the dashboard in your car, in the opening of your wallet on a post-it-note, on your bathroom mirror, or even make them your screen saver. Repeat your way to success!

CLEAR OUT LIMITING BELIEFS

The only thing keeping you from what it is you want is the story you have about why you cannot have it. For example, if you think you will never get a high-ranking position, you will not. If you think you will never have a job you truly love, that pays well, and where your boss and co-workers appreciate your talents, you will not take the steps needed to find that job.

Luckily, your imagination is a **POWERful** tool. Use it to achieve your goals. Visualize your cubicle to be a corner office with a view, your paycheck big enough to cover all your expenses and more, and holding a business card with your dream title on it.

Create supernatural deposits in your life by starting every day on a positive note. Do this by repeating affirmations. By repeating positive things about yourself, you vanish negative thoughts from your life and find yourself with deep reserves of goodwill, hope, enthusiasm, and optimism.

You are what and where you are today because of words you have spoken during your life. The more you speak with belief and passion and take action, the quicker your goals will become a reality.

Shifting beliefs takes work, remember, even if you work hard to do things in a new way, be aware of any lingering beliefs and be honest enough with yourself to write them down.

Remember, too, that you are unique. No one else possesses the exact set of skills and life experiences you do. No one can do as good a job at being you as you can. If you allow yourself to be "you," there is no way you can fail. For that to prove true you must rid yourself of any negative beliefs you have about yourself.

In Anthony Robbins's classic book *Awaken the Giant Within,* he states, "Beliefs have the awesome potential to create or destroy... Learn to choose the beliefs that **emPOWER** you; create convictions that drive you in the direction of [your] destiny."

Most roadblocks to success are psychological. You can either be your own best friend or your own worst enemy. You can choose to say positive things to yourself or sabotage your success with negative words and beliefs. As Henry Ford once said, *"Whether you believe you can or believe you can't, you're probably right."*

The beliefs you have about yourself are entirely up to you, and they greatly influence your ability to be successful. If you believe, for instance, that you are successful and talented and that you have the staying **POWER** necessary to complete any task you set out to accomplish, you will be much more likely to live that reality. But if you hold tight to limiting beliefs about yourself-for instance, if you see yourself as unexperienced or uneducated you will not have as much confidence to help you weather challenges and come out successful.

Your beliefs about yourself are entirely in your control. You can choose to believe whatever you want about yourself, make a conscious decision right now to believe the best of yourself. The first step is identifying the limiting beliefs you have about yourself and your potential and recognizing that they are not fact, they are simply a story you have been telling yourself.

Give Yourself a BOOST: Identify the Limiting Beliefs

It is time to identify up to ten limiting beliefs that you hold about yourself, so you can acknowledge their existence as a first step in letting them go. Here are some examples of limiting beliefs:

- This is the best I can do.
- I cannot start over.
- It is not going to get any better; it is what it is.
- I will never get a promotion.
- I will never find the right job.
- I will never get a big break.
- I am not very smart.
- I can't finish anything.
- I will never get what I want.
- I am not good enough.
- No one cares if I succeed.
- I am destined to fail at everything I try.
- No matter how hard I try, I will never have the career I dream of.
- There is too much competition; I could never measure up.
- It is too hard for me to change.

- It is too late for me to change.
- If I have not succeeded by now, I never will.
- I do not have the brains/looks/skills/connections I need to excel in my dream job.
- I am cursed; I am doomed to fail.
- Everything they said about me was right; I am just no good.
- I am a failure.
- I am a slacker.
- Life sucks and so do I.
- I am a procrastinator who will never amount to anything.
- I am too messed up to achieve my goals.
- I have done too many things wrong to make things right.
- Life never goes my way.
- I have terrible luck.
- I do not have the connections I need to succeed, so I may as well not try.
- I do not have the education/qualifications to succeed, and I never will.
- I cannot commit to anything.
- If only I had listened back then, I could have succeeded. Now my chance has passed.

In the following box, identify up to ten limiting beliefs about your personal abilities and attributes that have kept you from following through on goals or aspirations. You can use any from the list above, but also consider any that run through your head whenever you feel stressed or challenged or when you imagine starting something new. As you list your limited beliefs, have compassion for yourself. Often we develop limiting beliefs about ourselves as a way to protect ourselves from trying something and then suffering the pain, rejection, or humiliation of failure. While it is a good impulse to try to protect yourself, the problem with this particular method is that you will be guaranteed to suffer all the pains you are most afraid of, because your beliefs will ensure the very failures and pains you are trying to avoid.

Limiting Beliefs
1.
2.
3.
4.
5.
6.
7.
8.
9.
10.

Give Yourself a BOOST: Instill Positive Beliefs

The next step in renovating your belief system is to consciously work on instilling positive beliefs about yourself. Ideally, you will choose beliefs that directly replace your negative beliefs. Here are some examples:

- I learn anything I set my mind to.
- I finish anything I start.
- I get what I want.
- I am good enough, just as I am.
- My success benefits many people.
- I am destined to succeed at whatever I try.
- My efforts earn me my dream career.
- I have unlimited potential.

- I have as much chance to succeed as anyone else.
- I change my habits and my beliefs with ease.
- I have all the time in the world to achieve my goals.
- I continue to try and therefore I succeed.
- I have the brains/looks/skills I need to excel in my dream job.
- I am blessed; I am destined to succeed.
- Every positive thing they say about me is right; I am a very good person.
- I am a success
- I am a diligent worker.
- I enjoy being on top of things and my efforts pay off.
- My unique set of experiences and challenges will help me achieve my goals.
- I learn from my mistakes and transform them into great results.
- Life is going my way.
- I have good luck.
- I make every day a great day.
- I am a star.
- I develop the connections I need to succeed.
- I gain the education/qualifications I need to rise higher.
- I enjoy committing to activities that nourish me and advance my dream career.
- My past has led me to where I am today and I am perfectly positioned to achieve the career of my dreams.

In the following box, identify ten positive beliefs about your personal abilities and attributes that will support you in following through on your goals and aspirations. You can use any from the list above, but feel free to dream up exactly what you would like to hear and think whenever you feel stressed or challenged or try something new.

Put these positive beliefs somewhere you will see them and repeat them to yourself-slowly and thoughtfully-several times a day. First thing in the morning and right before bedtime are ideal times to repeat these new positive beliefs. Soon you will also find them popping into your mind when you need them most and they will support you on your way to achieving your full potential.

Positive Beliefs
1.
2.
3.
4.
5.
6.
7.
8.
9.
10.

Give Yourself a BOOST: Reframing the Past

We all have mistakes or setbacks that threaten to undermine our faith in our potential. By reframing these events into an **emPOWERing** learning experience, you make new conclusions about what is possible for you. First read the example that follows, and then **fill** in the blanks to reframe lessons about some of your past regrets.

What was the incident?

I got fired from a great job. While this job was not helping me move toward my dream job, it paid well, and I liked some things about it. Still, my heart was not fully in it, and my lack of enthusiasm caused me to make mistakes. My boss noticed this and I was fired.

What did I learn from this incident?

I learned that I need to make sure I take a job I feel truly enthusiastic about. If I have to take a job that is not on the path to my dream career, I need to see it as temporary and continue steadily working toward my dream career. I also learned that when I am not excited about my job, it is not fair to my employer, or me and it leads to hard feelings and disappointments on both sides, and I learned that just because something is "a great job," it does not mean a job is great for me.

What must I change now and why do I know I can do it?

From now on, I will make sure that I am always doing something tangible toward getting my ideal career. If at all possible, I will take work only in my desired field. If I need to take a different job to support myself financially, I will make sure I am simultaneously and consistently building my skill set and applying for other jobs in my desired field

What are three ways to get myself out of the limiting beliefs that led me to this situation?

1. *I will remind myself every time I think about getting fired that I learned some great lessons from that experience, and that I will not repeat the same mistakes again.*
2. *When I make my **S.M.A.R.T.** goals and my Mission Statement later in this book, I will make sure I am working hard toward acquiring a job I am genuinely excited about.*
3. *I will allow myself to see how this experience, as painful as it was, helped further me on the path to my dream job.*

Now that you have read the example, do this for three of your past experiences that felt the worst or that bothered you the most. While it can be painful to revisit these experiences, doing so in this exercise helps you face the truth of the past and use it to your best advantage in the future.

Reframing the Past #1

What was the incident?

_____

_____

_____

_____

What did I learn from this incident?

_____

_____

_____

_____

What I must change now, and why do I know I can do it?

_____

_____

_____

_____

What are three ways to get myself out of the limiting beliefs that led me to this situation?

1.

_____

_____

_____

2.

_____

_____

_____

3.

_____

_____

_____

Reforming the Past #2

What was the incident?

_____

_____

_____

_____

What did I learn from this incident?

_____

_____

_____

_____

What I must change now, and why do I know I can do it?

_____

_____

_____

What are three ways to get myself out of the limiting beliefs that led me to this situation?

1.

_____

_____

_____

2.

_____

_____

_____

3.

_____

_____

_____

Reframing the Past #3

What was the incident?

_____

_____

_____

What did I learn from this incident?

_____

_____

_____

_____

What I must change now, and why do I know I can do it?

_____

_____

_____

_____

What are three ways to get myself out of the limiting beliefs that led me to this situation?

1.

_____

_____

2.

_____

_____

3.

_____

_____

_____

GETTING RID OF "SHOULDS"

"Shoulds" are all the things we tell ourselves we should do. For example:

- I should go back to school.
- I should be rich by now.
- I should be in a better financial position right now.
- I should get a job that is more rewarding.
- I should list all the things I want to accomplish and set firm deadlines.
- I should stop procrastinating.

The list goes on and on. The problem with "shoulds" is that they are critical and judgmental statements that do not inspire us. They make our dreams feel like tasks. Most insidiously, "shoulds" do not actually challenge us to do anything-they just point out what we haven't done.

That is why you must change all your "shoulds" into "I wills." "I will," challenges you to commit to do something; it reminds you that you can do it and how much you want it and inspires you to feel like it is possible.

Give Yourself a BOOST: Turn Your "Shoulds" into "I Wills"

Make a list of all the things you should do (or "should have" done):

1. _____

2. _____

3. _____

4. _____

5. _____

6. _____

7. _____

8. _____

9. _____

10. _____

Now transform those "should" into I wills (go ahead—rewrite them):

1. _____

2. _____

3. _____

4. _____

5. _____

6. _____

7. _____

8. _____

9. _____

10. _____

You can use this list to help you set your **S.M.A.R.T.** goals in the next chapter. For now, just allow yourself to enjoy being rid of all those awful "shoulds!"

Give Yourself a BOOST: Conquer Your Fears of Success

It is very common for people to fear pursuing success. We may have been shamed for making mistakes and therefore fear trying, somewhere along the line, we may have been taught that actively pursuing our own success is selfish. Perhaps we experienced ridicule firsthand or witnessed others being humiliated by defeat, rejection, failures, or disappointments. These kinds of experiences, if left unaddressed, cause us to become **disemPOWERed.** That is the risk if we put too much faith in the opinions of others who do not encourage us to pursue our dreams. The fact is, there will always be something or someone who can deter us from our goals if we let them. Instead, make the decision today to conquer your fears of success and allow yourself to move forward.

Life allows you to be challenged to learn and grow. Throughout your journey you have the opportunity to make changes in your attitude and behavior and become more skilled and **POWERful.** If you complete the action steps recommended you will immediately begin to think differently about:

- Your personal **POWER**
- Your fears
- Your standards and your words
- Your ability to reach goals
- Your vision for success

Everyone has potential, even if they cannot identify their unique or natural abilities in a given area. In fact, potential and value were built into all of us from the time we were born. You have great talents, abilities, and skills that, if developed and used, will allow greater possibilities to become available to you.

Successful people tend to oversimplify their good qualities and consider their inaccuracies as unique occurrences. For example: *I do well at public speaking, so I will do well at anything.* Less accomplished people tend to do the opposite: *I am terrible at standing before a group of people and speaking, so I will be bad at facilitating leadership meetings and I could never get a job higher than an entry-level position.*

Successful people know they do not have to wait to master every skill before they jump into the game of life. We do not learn by being perfect. One of the best ways to tackle our fears and **POWER** our potential is to get in the game and master it through practice. We just need to start where we are right now and build from there. It is fear that causes us to generalize from one setback that we will not succeed at future endeavors, but as long as we continue to let ourselves believe we will not succeed we will continue to fall short of our dreams.

Fear is commonly defined as False Evidence Appearing Real. Fear can be crippling and often stops us from living up to our fullest potential. Fear makes us believe that everyone else is better, brighter, more **POWERful,** and more talented than we are and that we really do not deserve to be successful. Fear of success can result in guilt, confusion, or anxiety when we do achieve success. These feelings can lead you to chronic underachievement and eventually cause us to lose our momentum.

Make a commitment to yourself right now to develop new behavior patterns to overcome your fear of success and use the steps in this book over and over again for revisiting and monitoring your level of commitment and motivation to reach your goals. It strengthens, **emPOWERs,** and reinforces the hard work, effort, and sacrifices you have made to achieve success. It also gives others in your life permission to give you honest, open, and candid feedback when they see you self-destructing or backsliding. Most importantly it allows you to awaken the real you.

Give Yourself a Triple BOOST: Conquer Your Fears

Answer the following questions to uncover your fears and to understand them, and then balance them with positive feelings about your pursuit of happiness and success.

What do you fear the most about pursuing your dream job?

_____

_____

_____

_____

Negative outcomes you imagine:

_____

_____

_____

_____

What would the positive outcomes look like without the presence of those fears?

_____

_____

_____

_____

Fear is an emotion and can be controlled just like your ability to control crying or laughter. I am sure you or someone you know has experienced a time when they were laughing hysterically and had to cut it off quickly, and was able to do so, when someone walked in the room. Have you ever gotten really emotional to the point of tears while watching a sad movie and had to pull yourself together before answering an important call. Guess what? Your fears can be controlled the same way. Fear and the perceived consequences of your fears holds no more **POWER** than you give to them.

Think of one fear that you have about succeeding in your career and begin shifting your actions toward one of the positives on your list above. Make a conscious effort to concentrate on knocking down the inner walls of fear in your mind so you can confidently **POWER** your path to ultimate success and satisfaction.

Day 4

Set S.M.A.R.T. Goals

"The reason most people never reach their goals is that they do not define them or ever seriously consider them as believable or achievable.
Winners can tell you where they are going, what they plan to do along the way, and who will be sharing the adventure with them."

-Denis Watley

Day 4

Set S.M.A.R.T. Goals

If there were no restraints and you knew you could not fail, what would you set out to accomplish? Goal setting is a **POWERful** tool, and it allows you to track your progress as you strive to enhance your professional life. Also, according to the law of attraction, you attract to your life whatever you give your attention, focus, and energy to, whether it is what you want or what you do not want. By setting goals around your dream career, you will attract opportunities and circumstances that help you reach your professional potential.

As you set goals, do not limit yourself because you lack education or experience-you can always include getting more education or experience in your goals. You can accomplish any goal you set your heart and mind to, so dig deep and aim high.

Give Yourself a BOOST: State Your Basic Goals

After reviewing your assessments from day 1 (including your BOOST CAMP Analysis, Transferable Skills Inventory and Transferable Skills Statements, your **S.T.A.R.** statements, and your entries to the list "Keeping Track of the Skills You Want to Build"), make a list of all of your goals around your professional life. For example:

- Get a job that allows me to spend more time with my family
- Earn a promotion that will allow me to earn more money
- Learn a new line of work
- Earn an advanced degree in my field
- Retire in ten years
- Pursue a career that aligns with my passion
- Get a job that feels meaningful to me
- Get a job in a supportive/exciting workplace
- Work from home
- Have a commute no longer than fifteen minutes

Each of your goals should be written in one positive sentence (for example, rather than "stop commuting" you might write "work from home," and instead of "quit my job," you might write "get a new job as a virtual accounting assistant").

Did you know that 3% of the population has *specific, written* goals?

As a result of goal setting...

They are 10 times more likely to achieve their goals than:
- 10% of the population that have general, unwritten goals,
- 37% of the population that just dream and wish, and
- 50% of the population that wait for things to happen to them!

Goal #1

_____

_____

_____

Goal #2

_____

_____

_____

Goal #3

_____

_____

_____

Goal #4

_____

_____

_____

CHOOSE AN ACCOUNTABILITY PARTNER

Having an accountability partner dramatically increases your chances for success. Tens of thousands of corporate professionals at all levels and numerous major sports figures and athletes rely on business and personal development coaches to support their success. An accountability partner can be a family member, a very close friend, or a mentor you admire and with whom you have regular contact. It can also be a personal coach or a therapist who supports your progress and goals. Ideal accountability partners are people who genuinely support your mission, who enjoy being a part of your success, and who will not shame you but will excuse you when you have setbacks along the way.

It is natural for you to want to come across as a success to those who care about you and to want to avoid letting someone down by being less than true to your word. When you make a commitment to an accountability partner to spend five hours researching schools or companies, you are more likely to do it because you want to show that person you're a success. You also get the added bonus of feeling accompanied on your journey, which helps alleviate loneliness and allows for you to be appreciated for each successful step you make along your journey.

It is important that this person has a clear picture of your success plan and knows exactly what it takes to keep you motivated or knows just what to do or say to get you back on track quickly. Similar to a trainer at a gym, an accountability partner acts as your personal **"emPOWERment"** coach for your career. If possible, it is great to choose someone who is more advanced in your field, but it is most important that this person be someone with whom you are willing to share your high and low points. Choose someone who is a good listener and who can provide a safe haven for your concerns and be a valuable sounding board for your plans.

Give Yourself a BOOST: Finding Your Accountability Partner(s)

The last step in building your network is to choose an accountability partner who will support your success by giving you someone to report on the deadlines you have set for yourself.

First, call or email your first choice of accountability partners. If it seems appropriate, let this person know that you have been working through this book and that you are looking for an accountability partner to help you stay on track with your action plan. Ask if she or he would be willing to hear what would be involved and then consider playing that role in your goals.

Then share with this person your **S.M.A.R.T.** goals (including why you want to achieve them) and your Mission: Possible Statement and ask, "Would you be willing to be my accountability partner?" Explain what this would involve (having a copy of your goals and deadlines, expecting a weekly progress report by e-mail from you and an e-mail or call on the date of any deadlines with a report on how things went; celebrating with you when you accomplish each goal; encouraging you each time you get discouraged).

If the person is on board, give him or her a copy of your Leadership **B.O.O.S.T.** analysis, your **S.T.A.R.** stories, your **S.M.A.R.T.** goals, your Mission: Possible Statement, and your Action Plan (which you will create on day 7). Put it in a nice folder, so your accountability partner can refer to these things as needed. Put the action plan in front and highlight the dates of all the upcoming deadlines. Include contacting your accountability partner as part of each action step.

Thank your new accountability partner profusely. Perhaps offer the same support for your partner if he or she ever wants to accomplish a goal. Remember to send your accountability partner periodic thank-you cards and little treats, and remember to thank him or her every time the two of you speak. As you reach each milestone, send something special as a thank you (such as flowers, a gift certificate for a nice restaurant or favorite bookstore, a weekend at a local bed and breakfast, a round of golf at a favorite country club or something else that shows how much you appreciate the support).

Give Yourself a Double BOOST: Turn Your Goals into S.M.A.R.T. Goals

The Chances of successfully achieving your goals dramatically increase when you set goals using the **S.M.A.R.T.** principles: Specific, Measurable, Attainable, Realistic, and Timed goals.

A ***S.M.A.R.T. goal is Specific.*** It provides a clear picture of the goal and well-defined actions to perform-increasing the likelihood of achieving success.

For example: If your goal is to make a lot of money, what does that mean to you? How much exactly do you want to earn?

- A **S.M.A.R.T.** goal in this area would include a specific dollar amount. It would also include important reasons why you want to achieve this goal. For example: I want to earn $80K annually, so I can pay off all outstanding debt and save for a down payment on my dream house near the beach.

A *S.M.A.R.T. goal is Measurable.* It is phrased in a way that allows you to measure your progress and know when you have succeeded. Measuring actions and progress can be an excellent motivator.

For example: If your goal is to learn a new line of work, a **S.M.A.R.T.** version of that goal might be:

- Spend five hours per week for the next three months researching career options, aptitude tests, performing Internet research, and taking informational interviews.

A *S.M.A.R.T. goal is Attainable.* Setting goals that you can reach gives you confidence. Once you reach that goal, you can continue setting goals that slowly get you where you want to be. Is the goal attainable within the established time frame?

For example: It is important to break goals down into components that you can attain in a reasonable amount of time, so that you can use your accomplishments to fuel your continued progress. If your goal is to be president of the United States, a **S.M.A.R.T.** version of this goal might be as follows:

- Volunteer for a political campaign in the next election cycle, taking on as much responsibility as possible so that I can learn the process to better prepare for the running of local office in the following election.

A *S.M.A.R.T. goal is Realistic.* Goals should have an element of risk or growth, but they should be only slightly out of your grasp, challenging you to grow without causing you to feel defeated before you start.

For example: If your goal is to become a teacher and you have never taught nor do you have the educational background needed to teach, it would not be realistic to expect yourself to become a teacher in three months. A **S.M.A.R.T.** version of this goal might be as follows:

- Enroll in a credentialing program this year, complete the program in two years, and then apply for all available teaching positions in your area.

S.M.A.R.T. goals are Timed. Goals without deadlines risk being shifted aside from whatever seems pressing at the moment. Also, setting a timeframe allows you to evaluate your progress and restate your goals accordingly. Without a deadline date, we often procrastinate.

For example: If your goal is to shorten your commute time, a **S.M.A.R.T.** version would be as follows:

- Find a new job with a commute time of no longer than fifteen minutes in the next six months.

Give Yourself a BOOST: Make Your Goals S.M.A.R.T.

For each of the goals on your list, complete the following exercise:

S.M.A.R.T. Goal #1

Original Goal:

_____

S.M.A.R.T. Goal

☐ Specific

_____

_____

_____

☐   Measurable

_____

_____

_____

☐   Attainable

_____

_____

_____

☐   Realistic

_____

_____

_____

☐   Timed

_____

_____

_____

Why do you want this?

_____

_____

_____

_____

_____

How will your reward yourself once the goal is achieved? (**Do not skip this step:** Rewards motivate us, and it is great to celebrate our achievements and efforts.)

_____

_____

_____

_____

_____

Your accountability partner will be:

_____

S.M.A.R.T. Goal #2

Original Goal:

_____

S.M.A.R.T. Goal

☐ Specific

_____

_____

☐ Measurable

_____

_____

☐ Attainable

_____

_____

_____

☐ Realistic

_____

_____

_____

☐ Timed

_____

_____

_____

Why do you want this?

_____

_____

_____

_____

_____

How will your reward yourself once the goal is achieved? (**Do not skip this step:** Rewards motivate us, and it is great to celebrate our achievements and efforts.)

BOOST Camp Tips for Setting S.M.A.R.T. Goals

- Be crystal clear about what you want
- Think through what you need to do to get it
- Set and prioritize your **S.M.A.R.T.** Goal list
- Execute your plan by doing something daily to bring you closure to your goal
- Track your progress
- Learn how to deal effectively with obstacles
- Pull from the knowledge of others as resources
- Cheerfully acknowledge your supporters
- Celebrate achievements

_____

_____

_____

_____

_____

_____

Your accountability partner will be:

_____

S.M.A.R.T. Goal #3

Original Goal:

_____

S.M.A.R.T. Goal

- ☐ Specific

_____

_____

_____

☐ Measurable

_____

_____

_____

☐ Attainable

_____

_____

☐ Realistic

_____

_____

_____

☐ Timed

_____

_____

_____

Why do you want this?

_____

_____

_____

_____

_____

_____

How will you reward yourself once the goal is achieved? (**Do not skip this step:** Rewards motivate us, and it is great to celebrate our achievements and efforts.)

BOOST Camp Tips for Setting S.M.A.R.T. Goals

- Be crystal clear about what you want
- Think through what you need to do to get it
- Set and prioritize your **S.M.A.R.T.** Goal list
- Execute your plan by doing something daily to bring you closure to your goal
- Track your progress
- Learn how to deal effectively with obstacles
- Pull from the knowledge of others as resources
- Cheerfully acknowledge your supporters
- Celebrate achievements

_____

_____

_____

_____

Your accountability partner will be:

_____

Continue to repeat the formula above until you reach these goals, then set new ones. Goal setting is a **POWERful** tool, and it allows you to track the progress of the decisions you make to enhance your life. Written goals:

- Give yourself a target to shoot for
- Provide motivation
- Keep your destination in sight
- Move you closer and closer to your dream career. As the old saying goes, "Failing to plan is planning to fail."

WRITE YOUR MISSION: POSSIBLE STATEMENT

Writing a professional mission statement can be a **POWERful** experience. By thinking through, clarifying, and writing down what you are working toward, you are less likely to get distracted, stuck, or thrown off course by setbacks.

There are a wide variety of ways to write a mission statement-from a company-wide perspective, from a start-up business perspective, from a personal perspective, or from a personal and professional perspective. In this case, you will be writing a professional mission statement, which may include some discussion of work/life balance. Ideally, in your statement, you want to be concise and clear and cover your broad purpose as well as your specific **S.M.A.R.T.** goals. In your mission statement, you will want to address the following questions:

What do you hope to accomplish?

What is your purpose in this endeavor?

Why is it important to you?

What are you committed to doing to achieve your goals?

What is your intended result?

The following is an example to help you get started:

Sample Mission Possible Statement

It is my mission to produce the highest-level of professional work, so that I will be promoted to a top-level leadership position in my field. It is important for me to have a leadership role in my field because 1) I enjoy leading and inspiring people to do their best work and take pride in themselves and their company; 2) I have a creative vision of how things can be streamlined and improved, and being in a leadership position will allow me greater **POWER** and flexibility to promote my vision; and 3) I am happiest when I support individual and team growth and have freedom and control in the projects I am working on.

I commit to working additional hours, taking continuing education classes, and seeking the assistance of several mentors in my field as a way to achieve my vision. I spend two hours at the beginning of each week reviewing my **S.M.A.R.T.** goals, planning out my week, checking in with my accountability partners to give them updates and get support and inspiration. I will remind myself of the importance of sticking to my highest mission. I post my plan where I can see it daily. I will not let a week go by without making some concrete progress toward my mission of advancing my career to a management position. I commit to celebrating every milestone.

In addition, I set aside at least one day a week to relax with family and friends. I take an hour a day and one full day each month to do self-care activities that have no purpose except to give me pleasure and rejuvenation, including reading magazines, watching movies, taking hikes, getting massages, and daydreaming/napping. I commit to living a well-rounded life that allows for great professional success as well as a loving connection with others and ongoing self-respect and self-care.

Give Yourself a BOOST: Write Your Mission: Possible Statement

In the space provided, write out your Mission Possible statement

_____

_____

_____

_____

_____

_____

_____

_____

Day 5

Build Your Dream Network

"Connect with positive people who are willing to celebrate in your vision towards a successful victory."

-Dr. Valerie D.W. James

Day 5

Build Your Dream Network

In order to achieve your full potential, you are going to need help from mentors, cheerleaders, support "staff," and peers striving alongside you, seeking to reach their own potential. By building your dream team, you ensure that you will have the guidance, love, and support needed to keep you inspired.

When selecting members of your dream network, choose carefully, based on who can be genuinely nurturing and supportive to you. Although unintentional, all advice is not good advice. Talking with certain people can leave you feeling listless, depressed, and drained. Psychologist, Jack Canfield, describes these people as *"energy vampires."* They suck all the positive energy out of you. Allowing yourself to listen to people who tear you down, cause you to doubt yourself, or undermine your goals and dreams can wear you down and stifle or even kill your dreams. Avoid sharing your dreams and aspirations with people who are not in the right place in their own lives to offer you genuine support and enthusiasm.

When you are around people who are positive, enthusiastic and supportive, you feel encouraged and inspired. You pick up their attitude, and you feel as if you have added strength to vigorously pursue your own goals. On this day, you will learn how to build and strengthen your support network.

ASSEMBLING YOUR DREAM TEAM

Your professional circle consists of the people you have worked over the years or have had close contact within your professional experiences, even if you have not spoken with them for a long time. Ideally, some of them will know what your professional talents and skills are and will be close enough to you to know what you do extremely well. Some will know your professional background and have some level of personal connection with you.

In addition, you may have friends and family members who are able to be a part of your professional support team, not because they necessarily know much about the specifics of your field, but because they know what stimulates and motivates you to do your very best and know your best qualities and strengths. These are the people who believe you can apply those skills to anything you take on. Having a balance of professional and personal connections on your dream team will allow you to get all kinds of support as you work towards actualizing your mission and achieving your full potential.

Give Yourself a BOOST: Taking Stock of Your Contacts

In this brainstorming exercise, you are going to list the names of every person you can think of with whom you have had contact. For now, write down everyone you think of. You can decide later who you will call or e-mail first. As you consider each question, think of leaders in your current work environment or, if you are in transition, go through every year of your adult life: every class, every job, every volunteer activity, every person you have met at a social or business function and include everyone who comes to mind.

Anyone you can call anytime and have an open and frank conversation about your job search (ask for advice, get support or inspiration, vent, etc.):

_____

_____

_____

Anyone you have not spoken with in a long time but with whom you could instantly reconnect at a deep level:

_____

_____

_____

Work colleagues you have felt close to:

_____

_____

_____

Family members and close friends who support your striving to reach your fullest professional potential:

_____

_____

_____

Exercise or hobby partners who are encouraging, caring or inspiring:

_____

_____

_____

People you have helped out in the past:

_____

_____

_____

Community leaders with whom you have a close connection:

_____

_____

_____

Former bosses, instructors and mentors (only those with whom you have had positive experiences):

_____

_____

_____

Former employees (yes, they can help, too):

_____

_____

_____

Any other people in your life who might be able to help in some way (paid or unpaid):

_____

_____

_____

Anyone with whom you have been out of touch for a while who might be able to help you (do not let any length of time stop you from reestablishing contact when you start your job search.

Everyone will have had to look for work at some point in their career, and most of them will be sympathetic and helpful), for example, family members, friends, and former teachers, mentors, former classmates.

_____

_____

_____

_____

_____

_____

You will be referring to these lists later in the chapter, when you build your networking plan. If you feel that you were not able to come up with enough truly helpful people, never fear-there is always time to strengthen and build your professional network. Even if you have a thriving network, you never know when a new contact might bring you just the training or opportunity you have been hoping to achieve.

Give Yourself a BOOST: Get Connected by Networking

Networking is a great way to expand your resources quickly. Here are some good options for networking events:

- Chamber of Commerce mixers
- Golf tournaments
- Business expos and conferences
- Service clubs such as Rotary and Kiwanis
- Trade and professional association meetings in your industry
- Professional Leadership Academy, lectures, workshops conferences and BOOST CAMP forms (see www. leadershipBOOSTcamp.com (for more information)

- Fundraisers hosted by educational institutions, community organizations and affinity groups
- Alumni associations for schools you have attended
- Social, cultural, and sporting events that include receptions or other mix-and-mingle time
- Private gatherings organized for the purpose of meeting new people and socializing
- Classmates in your field (often your classmates will have additional connections when you build positive relationships with others and mention what you're working toward, people may volunteer to put you in their network of contacts)

If you attend events that you deem worth your time, go back to the same groups regularly and become a familiar face. If you go to a group once and it does not seem like a promising environment, feel free to try other events until you find a few activities that suit you better. Professional association offers great resources and support and deepens your connections. Remember, it is not just about who you know, it is also about who knows you. Once you find two or three groups that have the right mix of people, get involved by volunteering your time and talent and be consistent with your efforts.

Networking is an awesome way for exchanging personal and professional talents, resources, and support. People you know will refer you to people they know, and sometimes those new acquaintances will refer you to others. If done regularly, networking allows you to create a pool of contacts from which you can draw business leads, referrals, creative ideas, and information for landing a job or progressing in your career.

It has been said that eighty-five percent of job seekers find work as the result of a referral from a friend or colleague, and only two-four percent land jobs from Internet job boards. Although networking takes time and effort, if used properly it is a

POWERful technique for making acquaintances of new people, building enjoyable relationships with like-minded people, and enhancing your confidence in reaching your goals.

Networking is also a great outlet for working through social anxiety. Almost everyone experiences symptoms of social anxiety from time to time. If you have a problem connecting with people in large or unknown groups, here are a few tips for overcoming your fears:

- Prepare for conversation. For instance, read the newspaper to identify an interesting story you can talk about and read your
- **S.T.A.R.** stories and your Mission Statement ahead of time so you can share with people what you have done and what you are working toward if they ask.
- Volunteer to do something you enjoy. Ideally, it will be something in your field. When you make connections with people outside of an office environment, they may be more likely to see you as a friend and as someone with whom they can exchange support and connections.
- Offer to help others in any way you can. They may be able to help you in the future, or good karma may just come to you for your good deeds.
- Make eye contact and greet each person you encounter.
- Strike up a conversation about new developments in the industry or comment on the event.
- Ask questions and show genuine interest in others' views experiences, and goals.
- When you encounter people with more success than you in your field, ask them out to lunch and discuss their thoughts about the field, learn about their path, and get their advice. This exchange often leads to someone becoming a contact.

When you encounter people with less success than you in your field, offer any support, advice, or encouragement that seems warranted. Networking is about exchanging support and ideas, not just about getting what you need from others.

Gradually repeating encounters such as these with three to five people at each engagement will improve your comfort level when participating in social activities and slowly expand your contacts. When others ask about you, be sure to offer your successes, what you are working toward and what you need (for example, "I am hoping to learn more about capital investments," "I am hoping to find a company that allows telecommuting," or "want to build alliances with others in my field").

Another great way to network is to plan lunch dates with current and former coworkers, alumni and personal friends. Do not shy away from reaching out to people you already know, even if you have been out of touch. Personal connections, that give you "hot leads" are a much more productive avenue for advancing your career than reading the want ads or surfing the Internet.

Give Yourself a BOOST: Make a Networking Plan

Research networking events in your area for at least an hour. You can find information on the Internet, in local or trade newspapers, through alumni associations from your past schools, and from colleagues. List three associations you would like to start with and the dates of their next event:

_____

_____

_____

_____

_____

_____

Whatever you do, remember to spend time with positive and supportive people. Who you associate with influences your thoughts, actions, and behaviors. When you are surrounded by supportive people, your energy level increases and you feel better about yourself, which helps to raise your self-esteem. Do not share your goals and dreams with people you know are going to be negative, unsupportive or fearful. Share your professional aspirations with people who are going to help **POWER** your potential.

Day 6

Take Care of Your Greatest Asset (You!)

"You are an asset to this world and your life matters. Make sure you treat yourself to some "ME" time. Include plenty of fun activities, pleasurable adventures, and relaxation in your life or you will compromise your sense of happiness and inner peace if you never find a time to laugh out loud and take care of your health."

-Dr. Valerie D.W. James

Day 6

Take Care of Your Greatest Asset (You!)

With increasing work demands and busy lifestyles, it can be easy to fail to pay attention to your physical and emotional health. You may tell yourself you are too busy to take care of yourself, but if afflictions take over and lead to poor health and fatigue it can lead to time off work, lost wages, and unfavorable perceptions of reliability if occurrences are frequent. It can also seriously compromise your sense of happiness and inner peace if you never take time to care for your health or make sure there is plenty of fun, pleasure, and relaxation in your life. To truly **POWER** your professional potential, you need plenty of energy, which comes from rest, relaxation, and enjoyment in all areas of life. In this chapter, you will learn how to prioritize yourself and your well-being as part of your plan for professional success.

Give Yourself a BOOST: Setting Aside One Hour a Day for You

Studies have shown that people who live out their potential and realize their dreams for professional success and satisfaction live longer than people who are just going through the motions.

To make this become real, you must create a pattern for doing more of what you enjoy by incorporating it into your life on a day-to-day basis. You deserve to live a life of satisfaction. If you enjoy long walks on the beach, get up earlier or end your day sooner. Pack your walking gear and change right before leaving work and head to the beach for a one-hour walk before going home.

Each day you must do something good for yourself-something you truly enjoy. Here are a few examples of things you might choose:

- Walk the dog at the beach or in the woods
- Soak in the bathtub with a magazine
- Take golf lessons
- Take a dance or yoga class, go for a swim, or do some other kind of physical activity that helps you get fit and feel centered
- Cook yourself a healthy meal that you really enjoy (you can count this only if you genuinely enjoy cooking!)
- Lie on the grass and watch the clouds
- Go fishing
- Participate in water aerobics
- Read a book at a cafe
- Talk to a favorite friend or relative on the phone
- Watch a favorite TV show or sporting event
- Listen to music
- Take a nap
- Get a massage (or give yourself a foot rub)
- Cuddle with your sweetheart or pet
- Paint, draw, or otherwise express your creativity
- Play a musical instrument
- Meditate

Make a list here of the things that would be wonderful ways to spend your "You" hour each day. When you plan out each day, make sure you include one of these things on your day's schedule.

_____

_____

_____

_____

_____

_____

_____

_____

_____

Give Yourself a BOOST: Understand Your Personal Energy Level Body Rhythms

It is also important to understand your personal energy level body rhythms. For example, are you a morning person or does it take you a few hours before you can really engage in your work or in highly functional interactions with other? Below is an example of how you chart your personal energy level to improve effectiveness and efficiency in your work and interactions with other.

The image on the next page shows someone who is definitely a morning person. This person's personal energy level appears to be highest in the morning. He or she may get up every morning at 5:00am for a quick run and be in the office by 7:00am ready to engage in complex activities and discussion before 8:00am. The chart also shows that this person's personal energy level decreases after lunch and becomes even lower by the end of the day.

High: New learning, very complex activity

Good: Most activities

Average: Most activities, not highly complex or new learning

Below Average: Routine activities, attending meetings

Low: Easy activities, some routine activities

Compare your chart with several of your peers

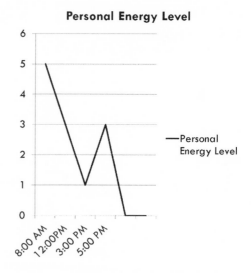

Circle the time of the day you feel you are the most focused

Morning   afternoon   evening   late night

Understand your personal energy level. Personal energy levels come from four main sources: the body, mind, feelings, and spirit. In each, energy can be systematically expanded and regularly renewed by establishing specific personal energy levels—behaviors that are intentionally practiced and precisely scheduled can make your everyday work engagement, activities and productivity consistent with what gives you a sense of meaning and purpose. Once you are aware of your level you can become even more productive by using the following tips as your guide.

Table XX shows best time to engage in activities during the time of the day your personal energy level is highest, good, average, below average, or low. Compare your chart with several of your peers. You will notice that your body rhythms may mirror each other or may be different.

Personal Energy Level Chart

Highest Energy	Good Energy	Average Energy	Below Average Energy	Low Energy
• New learning • Very complex activity	• One-on-one meetings or team meeting • Inspiring and productive conversations with your team and colleagues	• Project Planning and goals • Measure and monitor outcomes and result	• Routine administrative activities • Attending meetings	• Easy activities or checking emails • Some routine follow-up or review activities

Base on your identified peak body energy level write down activities you should be performing and at around what time of the day to become more effective in your daily life to avoid stress, procrastination and improve focus and efficiency at school, work and life. Note: you do not have to have to write an activate for every hour as some activities can be combined (Ex: If you are a morning person, you may be more focused and effective at completing your monthly report between 5am-7am or Studying for a critical mid-term exam between 7am-9am)

5 A.M.

_____

6 A.M.

_____

7 A.M.

_____

8 A.M.

_____

9 A.M.

_____

10 A.M.

---

11 A.M.

NOON

---

1 P.M.

---

2 P.M.

---

3 P.M.

---

4 P.M.

---

5 P.M.

---

6 P.M.

---

7 P.M.

---

8 P.M.

---

9 P.M.

_____

10 P.M._

_____

11 P.M.

_____

MIDNIGHT

_____

1 A.M.

_____

2 A.M.

_____

3 A.M.

_____

4 A.M.

_____

Give Yourself a BOOST: Taking Care of Your Physical Health and Well-Being

The only way you are going to reach your full potential is if you take really good care of yourself-getting plenty of sleep, allowing yourself to de-stress regularly, eating healthy meals, and getting regular exercise are crucial to your success. It is essential that you see your health as part of your plan for professional success. Being rested and healthy allows you to enjoy life more, think more clearly, and work more effectively. Make sure to include self-care in your action plan for success.

Here are a few ways to incorporate good health into your life:

- Visit the doctor for yearly checkups
- Eat plenty of healthy, fresh foods-especially fruits and vegetables every day
- Take a cooking class to learn healthy cooking and expand your network
- Get a minimum of twenty minutes of exercise each day (walk to work, walk around the neighborhood during your lunch break, join a gym, or take a fitness class that sounds really fun)
- Drink plenty of fresh water every day
- Wind down before bed and get at least six to eight hours of sleep each night
- Smile, laugh, and shower yourself with positive compliments and affirmations
- Tell yourself every day how proud you are of everything you have accomplished

Write here how you would like to take care of yourself. Remember to make these **S.M.A.R.T.** goals (Specific, Measurable, Attainable, Realistic and Timed). For example:

I am committed to cooking three healthy dinners each week and doubling the recipes so I will have healthy leftovers for at least three additional meals. I will join a weekend hiking club and go on one hike each week, in addition to walking to and from work three days a week. I will fill up a large container of water at the beginning of each day and drink all of it throughout the day. I will start and end each day by repeating to myself, "I really appreciate everything I am doing to take care of me."

_____

_____

_____

WEATHERING SETBACKS

Life throws everyone curves. No one goes through life without problems or without running into obstacles. What is important is how we face these obstacles. If we think negatively or come down hard on ourselves, we will become overwhelmed and ready to give up or become ineffective in dealing with the situation. Instead, we need to soothe ourselves with kind words and look for something positive in the situation. You can choose to consider it a blessing in disguise even if you have no idea at the moment what that blessing might be. Look for an advantage or opportunity in every situation. As Richard Bach points out in his book *Illusions,* ***"There is no such thing as a problem without a gift in its hands."***

When an unexpected problem arises I automatically say, "What am I to learn from this?" and then immediately look for the opportunity presented by the situation. Without a doubt I find it and move on.

Learning to deal successfully with obstacles can help you live a more fulfilling life. As Booker T. Washington said, *"Success is to be measured not so much by the position we have reached in life, as by the obstacles which we have overcome while trying to succeed."* Rather than seeing setbacks as a sign that you should give up, see setbacks as signs that you are moving forward and thus encountering one of life's inevitable obstacles. Seek out support from your accountability partners as well as others in your support network; learn from any mistakes you may have made, continue toward reaching your full potential.

REWARDING A JOB WELL DONE

Sometimes when you have got big plans, you can forget to commemorate all the successes you have had along the way. It is crucial to give yourself rewards and thanks for a job well done. The following is a list of small, medium and large rewards you can give yourself when you achieve a goal of equal magnitude (check any that appeal to you, and add as many as you would like and then do not forget to include these in your action plan when you complete the next chapter):

Small rewards for daily successes:

☐   Take an extra hour of "you" time spent any way you like

☐   Have dinner out with a friend

☐   Buy new golf equipment

☐   Meet a friend or two for happy hour

☐   Leave work an hour early (if permitted)

☐   Go to a movie

☐   Create a new play-list of your favorite songs

☐   Call a friend to share your success

☐   Pick up a favorite magazine

☐   Buy a new suit

☐   Take a long, hot bath/shower

☐   Let yourself "off the hook" with chores for the evening

☐   _____

☐ _____

☐ _____

☐ _____

☐ _____

Medium rewards for medium successes (Meeting weekly/monthly deadlines, successfully completing a **S.M.A.R.T.** goal, etc.):

☐ Get childcare so you and your partner can have a date night to celebrate your accomplishments

☐ Go away for a daytrip or a weekend

☐ Get a massage/facial/etc.

☐ Go to a sporting event/concert/play/musical

☐ Buy yourself a new outfit

☐ Go to a fancy restaurant you do not get to go to often

☐ Go on a long hike/bike ride some place beautiful

☐ Write an e-mail to share your success with loved ones

☐ _____

☐ _____

☐ _____

☐ _____

☐ _____

Big rewards for accomplishing major goals (getting a new job/promotion, earning a degree or certificate in your field, accomplishing all of your **S.M.A.R.T.** goals, reaching your mission, etc.):

☐   Go on a long vacation to somewhere you have always wanted to go

☐   Have a spa weekend with a friend or all by yourself

☐   Take a series of weekend trips (perhaps one each month for a year)

☐   Throw a party and invite all your loved ones to celebrate your accomplishment

☐   Write a letter to yourself telling yourself all the things you have done well and all of the reasons you are proud of yourself

☐   Take a weekend away by yourself to plan your next set of **S.M.A.R.T.** goals and revise your Mission: Possible Statement

☐   Buy yourself season tickets to your favorite live performance/sporting event

☐   Get a makeover so that your outside matches your inside

☐   _____

☐   _____

☐   _____

☐   _____

☐   _____

Celebrate YOU!

Day 7

Create Your Action Plan

"Make and sign a POWER to THRIVE contract with yourself for the goal you want to accomplish and see the POWER of your fullest potential soar."

-Dr. Valerie D.W. James

Day 7

Create Your Action Plan

Small, consistent action over time produces results. It is crucial that you align your habits with the vision of how you desire to become and the goals you want to accomplish. Your habits must support behaviors that allow you to **POWER** your potential to thrive.

To actualize your goals you must have a plan. A plan is an outline in writing that offers inspiration, and motivation and keeps you on track.

Using your **S.M.A.R.T.** goals and your Mission: Possible Statement, it is time to write out the actions you need to achieve your fullest potential. Put the steps in order, make a commitment to doing them regularly, do not let outside circumstances stop you, and you will have the career you have always dreamed of!

Give Yourself a BOOST: Write Your Action Plan

Write at least the first ten action steps to be taken towards your professional potential. Once step 1 is completed, cross it off of your list then move to the next one and keep repeating the steps. Success breeds success. Each time you accomplish a goal, you send a message to your brain that you are a success, which fuels you to continue succeeding.

Most likely your action plan will involve more than ten steps. Once you have completed this plan, make sure you send a copy to your accountability partner.

117

POWER Your Potential BOOST CAMP

Greatest Professional Goal:

_____

_____

_____

_____

_____

Step 1:

_____

_____

_____

Deadline:

_____

Reward:

_____

☐ Completed
☐ Contacted Accountability Partner
☐ Reward Granted

Step 2:

_____

_____

_____

Deadline:

_____

Reward:

☐ **Completed**
☐ **Contacted Accountability Partner**
☐ **Reward Granted**

Step 3:

Deadline:

Reward:

☐ **Completed**
☐ **Contacted Accountability Partner**
☐ **Reward Granted**

Step 4:

Deadline:

Reward:

☐ Completed
☐ Contacted Accountability Partner
☐ Reward Granted

Step 5:

_____

_____

_____

Deadline:

_____

Reward:

_____

☐ Completed
☐ Contacted Accountability Partner
☐ Reward Granted

Step 6:

_____

_____

_____

Deadline:

_____

Reward:

_____

☐ Completed
☐ Contacted Accountability Partner

☐ **Reward Granted**

Step 7:

_____

_____

_____

Deadline:

_____

Reward:

_____

☐ **Completed**
☐ **Contacted Accountability Partner**
☐ **Reward Granted**

Step 8:

_____

_____

_____

Deadline:

_____

Reward:

_____

☐ **Completed**
☐ **Contacted Accountability Partner**
☐ **Reward Granted**

Step 9:

_____

_____

_____

Deadline:

_____

Reward:

_____

- ☐ Completed
- ☐ Contacted Accountability Partner
- ☐ Reward Granted

Step 10:

_____

_____

_____

Deadline:

_____

Reward:

_____

- ☐ Completed
- ☐ Contacted Accountability Partner
- ☐ Reward Granted

TAKE THE FIRST STEP

It is always best to start something while you are feeling inspired, take the time right now to complete step 1 on your action plan. Go ahead-you can do it! You will feel fantastic knowing that you are already on your way to achieving your full professional potential and getting your dream career.

Give Yourself a Double BOOST: Imagine Yourself Living Your Dream

You do not have to wait until your goal has been accomplished to enjoy the good feelings you will get from reaching your full potential. All you have to do is close your eyes and imagine yourself living your dream. Visualize your daily life; feel how your body feels when you have succeeded in your goals and moved forward in your life. Doing this visualization regularly fuels you to keep going and allows you to feel the wonderful feelings of success all along your journey.

Give Yourself a Double BOOST: Visualize Your Life One Year from Now

Imagine your life one year from now, after you have successfully completed the first 20%, 50% or 100% of your goals in your action plan. Imagine how your life has changed. See yourself walking, talking, and interacting from that place of success. Allow yourself to feel how your body feels being such an amazing success. Do your muscles feel more relaxed? Are you more energized? When you allow yourself to fully imagine your dream, you automatically are strengthened and inspired to take more steps toward it. So many times, we give up our headspace to picturing the worst-case scenarios-but no more. It is time to picture the best-case scenario: You, in your dream career, living your fullest potential.

Envision a life that is right for you. This is your potential. This is your dream. This is what you now have permission to believe in!

Give Yourself a BOOST: Make a Contract with Yourself

Putting things in writing makes us far more likely to do them. That is why businesses make people sign contracts: it makes the terms and the rewards clear, and inspires people to keep their word.

It is time to sign a contract with yourself. You will achieve your goals. **Giving up is not an option.** You will not give up. You will take good care of yourself, reward yourself, reach out for help, and comfort yourself during adversities. You promise yourself you are going to come through for yourself this time-because you are going to **POWER** your potential and thrive.

Give Yourself a Triple Double BOOST: Write and Sign Your POWER to THRIVE Action Contract

_____

_____

_____

_____

I am committed to this action because:

_____

_____

_____

_____

_____

_____

_____

_____

Your Signature:

_____

Date:

_____

Accountability Partner's Signature:

_____

Date:

Life After BOOST CAMP

Life After BOOST CAMP

Congratulations on completing the ***POWER*** *Your Potential* **BOOST CAMP** Leadership Edition! First things first: go back to your rewards list and offer yourself a great reward for all the hard work you have done. Give yourself a pat on the back for taking your dreams seriously.

You now have a clear action plan, a host of **S.M.A.R.T.** goals, a Mission: Possible Statement, and some real clarity on your greatest accomplishments so far. Do not forget to gently toot your own horn at those networking events!

Now that **BOOST CAMP** is over and you have laid the groundwork for all your professional goals and aspirations to what is next? Here is a ten-step list to keep you on track:

1. Request to enroll in a half-day SMB School of Leadership **BOOST CAMP program** at www.leadershipboostcamp. com. It will help you further appreciate the new and more **POWERful** you as well as offer inspiration and additional resources for reaching your potential.
2. Review your action plan once a week (perhaps every Sunday evening or Monday morning), decide on the steps for that week toward achieving your goals, and email your

plans to your accountability partner.

3. E-mail your accountability partner a report at the end of the week, explaining what steps you took, how successful they were and ask for any support you need.

4. Reward yourself *every time* you take another step forward.

5. Once you complete the ten action steps on your action plan, write ten more action steps. Keep doing this until you have achieved all of your **S.M.A.R.T.** goals. If you run out of **S.M.A.R.T.** goals and you still haven't reached your end goal, take a few hours to write a new batch of **S.M.A.R.T.** goals. Update your action list and repeat.

6. Once you have reached your biggest goals and you are actively fulfilling your Mission: Possible vision daily. CELEBRATE!

7. After the celebration has died down and you have shared your success, settle into your dream job and enjoy!

8. When you start wondering again what is next for you (maybe in six months, a year, or five years), repeat this using your new experiences and skills to expand on your answers from the early chapters and set your new goals and dreams in the later chapter. Remember: **your potential is limitless!**

9. Support someone else in reaching his or her full potential. Buy a copy of this book for a loved one or colleague and become a mentor to someone in your field, because if there is one thing I have learned from this line of work, it is that nothing is as satisfying as helping **POWER** another person's potential!

10. E-mail your success story to me at: dr.valerie@ leadershipboostcamp.com. I **am your BIGGEST FAN and I would love to celebrate with you**

Remember...

*It is all about developing- "U," so take charge and **POWER** your potential to THRIVE!*

Lead Well, Your Mission is POSSIBLE!™

-Valerie D. W. James

BOOST CAMP
Leadership Resources and Recommended Reading

Anthony Robbins
Awaken the Giant Within

Valerie D. W. James
Leadership Intelligence Beyond the Basics

Diane Burke
Preparing for Your Interview

Ken Blanchard
The One Minute Manager

Nicholas Boothman
How to Connect in Business in 90 Seconds or Less

Donna Brooks
Seven Secrets of Successful Women

Julia, Mark and Cameron Bryan
The Artist's Way at Work

Marcus Buckingham
First, Break All the Rules

Dale Carnegie
How to Win Friends and Influence People

Jim Collins
Good to Great

Stephen Covey
Seven Habits of Highly Effective People

Richard Bach
Illusions

Jeffrey H. Gitomer
How to Connect in Business in 90 Seconds or Less

Michael D. Brown
Fresh Customer Service

Sarano Kelly
The Sales Bible

Malcolm Gladwell
Tipping Point

Sarano Kelly
The Game: Win Your Life in 90 Days

Patrick Lencioni
The Five Dysfunctions of a Team

John Maxwell
The 21 Irrefutable Laws of Leadership

Richard G. Shell
Bargaining for Advantage

Barbara Stanny
Secrets of Six-Figure Women: Surprising Strategies to Up Your Earnings and Change Your Life

John Wooden
My Personal Best

Ron Zemke
Delivering Knock Your Socks Off Service

Napoleon Hill
Think and Grow Rich

Leil Lowndes
How to Talk to Anyone: 92 Little Tricks for Big Success in Relationships

Danile, Fisher, Roger and Shapiro
Beyond Reason

Stephen Lundin
Fish!

Acknowledgements

To God be the glory! I would like to acknowledge my supportive husband and every person who has celebrated me in this journey. Without you, I would never have had the strength and faith to complete this book.

Mom, you are number one in my book. Thank you for being a great mom and best friend and a phenomenal example of resiliency. I had no idea that the ethical seeds you planted in my mental garden would shape my purpose in life as a woman, comrade, mother, and professional. Dad, thank you for being my biggest fan and instilling in me an entrepreneurial spirit, the tenacity to persevere with confidence no matter what the task may be and riding with me in the journey. I miss you Dad. I am so grateful to you, Ray, for making great deposits in my life as a wonderful parent and friend. Your compassion, unwavering love, support, and kindness have always made me feel larger than life.

I am so grateful for my children. Sir-Jonathan, thank you for your encouragement, good humor, and for making me feel like a STAR mom and for being my biggest fan. Michelle, thank you for your unconditional love and mental, physical, and emotional support in this journey. Brandon, thank you for encouraging me to stay fit and healthy.

Last but not least, to those of you who have ever doubted your inner POWER and outer excellence may you become an entrepreneur of self as you BOOST your career and POWER your Potential to THRIVE! and Lead Well!

About the Author

DR. VALERIE D. W. JAMES

Business Leader | International Speaker |Leadership Strategist |
Educator | Empowerment Coach

C lients, peers, former managers, and staff now call Dr. Valerie D. W. James the architect of accelerated learning, leadership and inclusion strategist for leaders, companies, and professionals that are ready to take their careers and organizations higher. Valerie is a human resources and management consultant in the corporate, healthcare, and higher-education arenas. Her advice is highly sought-after by current and future leaders, as well as C-level executives. Valerie has been studying, assessing, and researching organizational management and leadership practices since 1994. She has spent over two decades leading sales, service and human resources teams, using every aspect of her talent as a Beyond the Basics leader to achieve results personally and professionally. She has also served as president of a national human resources organization. In 1998, Valerie founded VisionSpot Consulting LLC, a corporate leadership, training, and organizational development firm with a national reach.

Valerie has partnered with thousands of leaders across the globe to strategize about people, process, and productivity enhancement, in addition to developing learning and development programs for all staff. She has successfully helped implement sustainable solutions that promote diversity, build inclusion, and transform the way leaders, individuals, and organizations work to achieve productivity results in utility companies and government and city agencies, as well as for-profit and nonprofit settings. She is well versed in assessing, hiring, training, and managing high performing teams from 2 to 200, as well as in organizations with more than 3,000 employees.

As a result, in 2009 Valerie founded the SMB School of Leadership BOOST CAMP®, a traveling institution that is dedicated to delivering evidence-based leadership development Solutions that Maximize Brilliance (SMB) among leaders and their teams. She also broadened the firm's brand to VisionSpot Consulting Group, LLC and widened their portfolio of services to include process improvement and project management strategies to increase operational efficiency in the workplace.

Valerie's aptitude for leadership effectiveness and process improvement strategies and techniques help expand the knowledge, growth, and engagement of employees at all levels. She has a deep understanding of leadership, human psychology, and motivation and will stretch beyond the reach of traditional leadership development programs to help you achieve tangible and measurable results. Valerie has received numerous leadership and service awards and accolades for streamlining processes, building continuity between leaders and their teams, and increasing customer and employee retention levels into the 80th percentile. These achievements have enabled VisionSpot to maintain and develop a company portfolio that consistently meets and exceeds clients' expectations.

Dr. Valerie D. W. James earned a doctorate in Education and Organizational Leadership from Pepperdine University. She is a Harvard trained leader, Six Sigma Green Belt Certified, a dynamic coach and speaker, and the author of three works: *Leadership Intelligence Beyond the Basics, POWER Your Potential BOOST CAMP®: 7 Days to Professional Success and Satisfaction, Leadership Behavior Practice Patterns' Relationship to Employee Work Engagement in a Nonprofit,* and *POWER Your Potential BOOST CAMP® Leadership Edition: 7 Days to Professional Success and Satisfaction,* Her name is synonymous with leadership, motivation, and success.

* * *

Dr. Valerie D. W. James can be reached for speaking engagements, complimentary consultations, and training programs and workshops at 310.704.0510–Cell | 866.970.1114 – Toll-Free | 888.479.2228 -Fax Dr.Valerie@leadershipboostcamp.com or via her website www.leadershipboostcamp.com

Made in the USA
Columbia, SC
31 May 2018